Policing to Promote the Rule of Law and Protect the Population

AN EVIDENCE-BASED APPROACH

Committee on Evidence to Advance Reform in the
Global Security and Justice Sectors

Committee on Law and Justice

Division of Behavioral and Social Sciences and Education

A Consensus Study Report of

The National Academies of
SCIENCES • ENGINEERING • MEDICINE

THE NATIONAL ACADEMIES PRESS
Washington, DC
www.nap.edu

THE NATIONAL ACADEMIES PRESS   500 Fifth Street, NW   Washington, DC 20001

This activity was supported by contracts between the National Academy of Sciences and the Bureau of International Narcotics and Law Enforcement Affairs of the U.S. Department of State, Award No. SINLEC20CA3213. Any opinions, findings, conclusions, or recommendations expressed in this publication do not necessarily reflect the views of any organization or agency that provided support for the project.

International Standard Book Number-13: 978-0-309-68535-1
International Standard Book Number-10: 0-309-68535-4
Digital Object Identifier: https://doi.org/10.17226/26217

Additional copies of this publication are available from the National Academies Press, 500 Fifth Street, NW, Keck 360, Washington, DC 20001; (800) 624-6242 or (202) 334-3313; http://www.nap.edu.

Copyright 2022 by the National Academy of Sciences. All rights reserved.

Printed in the United States of America

Suggested citation: National Academies of Sciences, Engineering, and Medicine. (2022). *Policing to Promote the Rule of Law and Protect the Population: An Evidence-Based Approach*. Washington, DC: The National Academies Press. https://doi.org/10.17226/26217.

The National Academies of
SCIENCES • ENGINEERING • MEDICINE

The **National Academy of Sciences** was established in 1863 by an Act of Congress, signed by President Lincoln, as a private, nongovernmental institution to advise the nation on issues related to science and technology. Members are elected by their peers for outstanding contributions to research. Dr. Marcia McNutt is president.

The **National Academy of Engineering** was established in 1964 under the charter of the National Academy of Sciences to bring the practices of engineering to advising the nation. Members are elected by their peers for extraordinary contributions to engineering. Dr. John L. Anderson is president.

The **National Academy of Medicine** (formerly the Institute of Medicine) was established in 1970 under the charter of the National Academy of Sciences to advise the nation on medical and health issues. Members are elected by their peers for distinguished contributions to medicine and health. Dr. Victor J. Dzau is president.

The three Academies work together as the **National Academies of Sciences, Engineering, and Medicine** to provide independent, objective analysis and advice to the nation and conduct other activities to solve complex problems and inform public policy decisions. The National Academies also encourage education and research, recognize outstanding contributions to knowledge, and increase public understanding in matters of science, engineering, and medicine.

Learn more about the National Academies of Sciences, Engineering, and Medicine at **www.nationalacademies.org**.

The National Academies of
SCIENCES • ENGINEERING • MEDICINE

Consensus Study Reports published by the National Academies of Sciences, Engineering, and Medicine document the evidence-based consensus on the study's statement of task by an authoring committee of experts. Reports typically include findings, conclusions, and recommendations based on information gathered by the committee and the committee's deliberations. Each report has been subjected to a rigorous and independent peer-review process and it represents the position of the National Academies on the statement of task.

Proceedings published by the National Academies of Sciences, Engineering, and Medicine chronicle the presentations and discussions at a workshop, symposium, or other event convened by the National Academies. The statements and opinions contained in proceedings are those of the participants and are not endorsed by other participants, the planning committee, or the National Academies.

For information about other products and activities of the National Academies, please visit www.nationalacademies.org/about/whatwedo.

COMMITTEE ON EVIDENCE TO ADVANCE REFORM IN THE GLOBAL SECURITY AND JUSTICE SECTORS

LAWRENCE W. SHERMAN (*Chair*), University of Cambridge Institute of Criminology
BEATRIZ ABIZANDA, Inter-American Development Bank
YANILDA MARÍA GONZÁLEZ, Kennedy School of Government, Harvard University
GUY GROSSMAN, University of Pennsylvania
JOHN L. HAGAN, Northwestern University
KAREN HALL, Rule of Law Collaborative, University of South Carolina
CYNTHIA LUM, George Mason University
EMILY OWENS, University of California, Irvine
JUSTICE TANKEBE, University of Cambridge Institute of Criminology

JULIE ANNE SCHUCK, *Study Director*
JESSALYN BROGAN WALKER, *Study Director (through June 2021)*
SARAH PERUMATTAM, *Senior Program Assistant*
EMILY P. BACKES, *Associate Director, CLAJ*
MEGAN SNAIR, *Technical Writer*

COMMITTEE ON LAW AND JUSTICE

ROBERT D. CRUTCHFIELD (*Chair*), University of Washington (*retired*)
SALLY S. SIMPSON (*Vice Chair*), University of Maryland
ROD K. BRUNSON, Northeastern University
SHAWN D. BUSHWAY, University at Albany
PREETI CHAUHAN, John Jay College of Criminal Justice
KIMBERLÉ W. CRENSHAW, University of California, Los Angeles
MARK S. JOHNSON, Howard University
CYNTHIA LUM, George Mason University
JOHN M. MACDONALD, University of Pennsylvania
KAREN J. MATHIS, American Bar Association (*retired*), University of Denver
THEODORE A. MCKEE, United States Court of Appeals for the Third Circuit, Philadelphia, PA
STEVEN RAPHAEL, University of California, Berkeley
LAURIE O. ROBINSON, George Mason University
CYNTHIA RUDIN, Duke University
WILLIAM J. SABOL, Georgia State University
LINDA A. TEPLIN, Northwestern University Medical School
HEATHER ANN THOMSON, University of Michigan
BRUCE WESTERN, Columbia University

NATACHA BLAIN, *Director*
EMILY P. BACKES, *Associate Director*

Preface

The movement for evidence-based policing in the 1990s came on the heels of the concept of evidence-based medicine in the same decade, but with far less clinical research to apply in policing practices. Since then, police research findings have been growing at a rapid rate and have been reviewed by the National Academies of Sciences, Engineering, and Medicine on repeated occasions in the last two decades. However, scant research findings have been reported at the country level, examining differences in police systems and policies across nations. In an era when the U.S. Congress has mandated better evidence to support public expenditure, the application of that mandate to overseas police development requires two responses. One is to do the best translation possible from existing research comparing differences between and within countries. The other is to map out research and action agendas that will promote the growth of new evidence to provide better guidance to policing in the international context.

This report is the first of five by a committee with diverse kinds of policing expertise assembled for the task by the National Academies. All five of these reports will be completed at the request of the Bureau of International Narcotics and Law Enforcement Affairs (INL) of the U.S. Department of State. The committee was charged by INL to identify good practices in police reform. INL's goal is for our reports to help ensure that ongoing U.S. foreign assistance for organizational police capacity building is informed by research. At the same time, INL seeks guidance from lessons learned from practitioners. Linking the two kinds of knowledge is an ongoing challenge in policing. Addressing this challenge requires a consensus-building process that identifies and then weighs the strength of relevant evidence, debates the conclusions, and engages a wide group of users to ensure that its presentation is relevant and accessible to them.

The project, beginning with this report, offers a unique opportunity to unite the research and practitioner perspectives for actionable recommendations that can strengthen the assistance provided for international policing.

In approaching my charge to chair this committee, I draw upon five decades of work in evidence-based police reform, partnering with police on five continents to both conduct research and apply it to policy making, with some successes and many failures. My own background is strengthened by a committee composed of experts across the areas of criminology, political science, economics, law, and international and organized crime. By joining in this undertaking, they have emphasized the need to draw from multiple fields to determine how policing can be improved. Committee members also bring with them a wealth of understanding from their work across Africa, Asia, Europe, Latin America, and North America. Their work has been intensely related to the various ways that communities experience the act of being policed and how police engage with their communities. This diversity of background led to robust discussions, not just about what can be concluded from existing evidence, but what the consequences might be from each recommendation we make. Our broadest area of agreement was the ongoing need for better evidence and infrastructure in each country for measuring the rule of law and harm to the public.

The report that follows considers the institutional landscape of policing and the capacity to provide proper and fair protection to all members of the public and not just to a powerful few. It examines organizational policies, structures, and practices for policing likely to be effective in some contexts at promoting the rule of law and protecting the population. We hope that for this broadest and perhaps most difficult of our five tasks, this report can provide a research agenda to better support program development in this area. The reader can use the report most wisely as a *provisional* statement of what is known, in 2021, on the basis of either systematic research evidence or case study experience. We fully expect some conclusions may change or that others may expand existing knowledge—especially with the research agenda we recommend.

While each report is published separately, all five should be seen as attempts to solve a larger puzzle of understanding and implementing successful police reform. This report offers a starting point for solving that puzzle.

Lawrence W. Sherman, *Chair*
Committee on Evidence to Advance Reform
in the Global Security and Justice Sectors

Acknowledgments

This report would not have been possible without the contributions of many people. First, we thank the sponsor of this study, the U.S. Department of State and the Bureau of International Narcotics and Law Enforcement Affairs, for requesting and supporting this endeavor. We have admired the sponsor's dedication to an evidence-led approach to further its programming.

Special thanks go to the members of the study committee, who dedicated extensive time, thought, and energy to this report. In addition to its own research and deliberations, the committee received input from several outside sources, whose willingness to share their perspectives and experience was essential to the committee's work. We thank Stephen White (Northern Ireland Human Rights Commission), Andrew Carpenter (United Nations Police Division), Elizabeth Linos (Goldman School of Public Policy), Anne Li Kringen (University of New Haven), Sir Denis O'Connor (University of Cambridge), and Gustavo Flores-Macías (Cornell University). The committee also gathered information through a commissioned paper. We thank Peter Neyroud (University of Cambridge) for his paper and for contributing both to the discussion at the committee's information-gathering workshop and to findings in the report.

The committee also wishes to extend its gratitude to the staff of the National Academies of Sciences, Engineering, and Medicine, in particular to Julie Schuck, who made critical substantive contributions in the conception, writing, and editing of the report, and Jessalyn Walker, who served as the study director until her departure in June 2021. Thanks are also due to Emily Backes who provided substantive writing and editing contributions and critical oversight and direction for the project. Sarah Perumattam provided key administrative and logistical support and made sure the committee process ran efficiently and smoothly. The National Academies Research Center, particularly Anne Marie Houppert, provided valuable research assistance. From the Division of Behavioral and Social Sciences and Education, we thank Kirsten Sampson-Snyder, who shepherded the report through the review process, and Douglas Sprunger and Dara Shefska, who assisted with the report's communication and dissemination. We also thank technical writer Megan Snair for quickly summarizing the presentations and discussions from the committee's workshop and editor Marc DeFrancis for their skillful writing and editing of the report manuscript.

This Consensus Study Report was reviewed in draft form by individuals chosen for their diverse perspectives and technical expertise. The purpose of this independent review is to provide candid and critical comments that will assist the National Academies in making each published report as sound as possible and to ensure that it meets the institutional standards for quality, objectivity, evidence, and responsiveness to the study charge. The review comments and draft manuscript remain confidential to protect the integrity of the deliberative process.

We thank the following individuals for their review of this report: Jay S. Albanese, Wilder School of Government and Public Affairs, Virginia Commonwealth University; Lucia Dammert, Humanities Department, University of Chile, Santiago; Andrew Faull, Justice and Violence Prevention Programme, Institute for Security Studies, Africa; Anna Giudice, Justice Section, Division for Operations, United Nations Office on Drugs and Crime; Liam O'Shea, Department of International Relations, London School of Economics and Political Science; and Victoria Walker, International Security Sector Advisory Team, Geneva Centre for Security Sector Governance, Switzerland.

Although the reviewers listed above provided many constructive comments and suggestions, they were not asked to endorse the conclusions or recommendations of this report nor did they see the final draft before its release. The review of this report was overseen by Alex R. Piquero, Department of Sociology and Criminology, University of Miami, and Philip J. Cook, Sanford School of Public Policy, Duke University. They were responsible for making certain that an independent examination of this report was carried out in accordance with the standards of the National Academies and that all review comments were carefully considered. Responsibility for the final content rests entirely with the authoring committee and the National Academies.

Contents

SUMMARY 1

1 INTRODUCTION AND OVERVIEW 13
  The Committee's Charge, 14
  Rule of Law, 18
  Evidence-Based Policing, 21
  Organization of the Report, 30

2 ORGANIZATIONAL STRUCTURES FOR POLICING 31
  Military vs. Civilian Forces, 32
  Governance of Police, 37
  Investigating Police Misconduct, 40
  Conclusion, 43

3 POLICIES FOR PROMOTING ACCOUNTABLE POLICING 45
  Police Recruitment, 46
  Appointment of Police Leadership, 52
  Use of Technology, 53
  Internal Governance, 58
  Conclusion, 61

4	**PROACTIVE POLICING PRACTICES**	63
	Problem-Oriented Policing, 65	
	Community-Oriented Policing, 69	
	Use of Discretion, 71	
	Conclusion, 73	
5	**CONCLUSIONS AND RECOMMENDATIONS**	75
	Translating the Evidence: Key Implications for Practice, 76	
	A Research Agenda for Evidence-Based Policing, 79	

REFERENCES   85

APPENDIXES
A Validation Exercise   95
B Biographical Sketches of Committee Members and Staff   103

Summary

The U.S. Department of State, through its Bureau of International Narcotics and Law Enforcement Affairs (INL), provides foreign assistance and supports capacity building for criminal justice systems and police organizations in approximately 90 countries around the world. It has a mandate to "strengthen fragile states, support democratic transitions, and stabilize conflict-affected societies by helping partner countries develop effective and accountable criminal justice sector institutions and systems."[1] With such a purpose, INL is part of a larger network of international and regional organizations, bilateral donors, international financial institutions, and civil society organizations that work in the broad area of police reform and capacity building in the security sector around the world. Like many donors, it strives to direct its resources to the most effective and efficient approaches to achieve its mission.

In 2018, guided by The Foundations for Evidence-Based Policymaking Act, INL created the Office of Knowledge Management to assemble evidence from research to inform its work. As part of the efforts to gather knowledge and improve its programs, INL asked the Committee on Law and Justice of the National Academies of Sciences, Engineering, and Medicine to convene an ad hoc committee to review, assess, and reach a consensus on existing evidence on policing institutions, police practices and capacities, and police legitimacy in the international context. A committee was assembled with expertise in criminology, economics, international and organized crime, law, policing, and political science.

---

[1] See https://www.state.gov/justice-programs-in-action.

The committee was tasked to produce a series of five reports addressing questions of interest to INL and the State Department. This report, the first in the series, is based on the question: *What organizational policies, structures, or practices (e.g., HR and recruiting, legal authorities, reporting lines, etc.) enable a police service to promote the rule of law and protect the population?* A commissioned paper and a workshop, structured by the committee to address the question, served as the primary sources of information for the committee's deliberations.

The complexity and magnitude of the challenges to learning "what works" in global organizational police reform are immense. While the science of policing outcomes has grown in recent years, it is limited in context, with much of the research conducted on policing taking place in the Global North countries (e.g., the United Kingdom and United States). It is also limited in purpose, with much research focused on examining crime reduction as opposed to examining the harms to the public as the result of crimes, violence, and any effects of policing activities.

There are contextual impediments to transferring this knowledge to policing in the Global South countries (i.e., the countries most likely to receive assistance from INL, such as those in Africa and Latin America). For the purpose of promoting the rule of law, impediments include differences in cultures and language, political regimes, legal systems, and the extent of political corruption in each country. Resistance to the rule of law by any element of the state can derail policing reforms, even when the knowledge and skills for reform are ready to deploy. In some places, that resistance can be violent and present harm to the public as well as police themselves who are engaging in reform efforts. When developing programs to assist with police reform, it is important to identify and make transparent the governance, labor, and political conditions that present barriers to sustained reform—whether they be under-resourced police agencies, forms of political repression, or an overlap between police and political elites and organized crime. With additional information, such consideration can help illuminate where and when it is feasible to proceed with any promising interventions, where it is best not to proceed, and where it is feasible to proceed but only with a plan for evading or overcoming any obstacles.

This report is written on the premise that there is opportunity to build on existing evidence. The generation of new knowledge should be directed toward informing the promotion of the rule of law and protection of the public across a variety of policing landscapes in different countries. This can be done, in part, by considering promising approaches, hypothesizing how they might be adapted for the local context, and deploying and evaluating interventions.

This report demonstrates the recent growth in policing research. It highlights preliminary findings on a range of topics, including some of the effects of various police structures, policies, and practices on some sets of outcomes. What continue to be missing from research in this area are evaluations of policing across different contexts and countries and standard measures of inputs, outputs, and how "effectiveness" might be measured across different agencies and contexts. To this end, the committee proposes an evidence-based approach to guide policing reform and interventions aimed at promoting the rule of law.

EVIDENCE-BASED POLICING

In the past two decades, a professional, social movement of "evidence-based policing" has spurred much research with the objective of applying knowledge to practice for the reduction of crime and protection of the public. Evidence-based policing is an approach to police practices and management that uses science and scientific processes to strengthen police decision making, actions, and overall agency functioning. At the core of an evidence-based approach to policing is the idea that actions, tactics, programs, and technologies used by the police should actually deliver the outcomes expected of them, ensuring accountable, effective, fair, and humane policing that seeks to minimize public harm and promote trust and legitimacy.

An evidence-based policing approach requires (1) a reliable body of knowledge about police practices; (2) the ongoing practice of evidence-based and systematic targeting, testing, and tracking in policing; and (3) the institutionalization and implementation of knowledge in police practices. As noted earlier, much existing knowledge from research focuses on the effects of policing approaches on crime prevention. However, a growing body of research also addresses evidence on such concerns as police efforts to improve relationships with the communities they serve; to improve trust and satisfaction in specific interactions with citizens; or to strengthen internal accountability mechanisms for rule-of-law policing. Notably, the development of this knowledge has required collaborations between researchers and police agencies.

A commitment to evidence-based policing requires agencies to actively and consistently test and evaluate their own practices against consistent standards. This is also true for donors, like INL, that are involved in promoting police reform. They should actively and consistently test and evaluate their investments and programs. In doing so, they will improve their knowledge management. Having high-quality information on crime, internal police functioning, and relevant public outcomes can then facilitate more accurate identification of problems and targeted solutions supported by evidence. The idea of evidence-based policing in contexts where record keeping is a low priority may seem unlikely to succeed, yet building the capacity to create and analyze records may be precisely the place to begin a global strategy of police reform. Gathering information is also a means to increase accountability, coordination, inclusion, and transparency.

Embedding research into practice requires fundamental adjustments to an organization's infrastructure, including, for example, management policies and technology. Evidence-based policing may also require legal frameworks and requirements to incentivize and institutionalize this approach in police agencies.

MEASURING THE RULE OF LAW

There are many working definitions for the rule of law (ROL). For this study, the committee leverages definitions from the United Nations and the U.S. State Department, but primarily it has considered how any definition of ROL could be turned into empirical measures.

> *A principle of governance in which all persons, institutions, and entities, public, and private, including the state itself, are accountable to [domestic] laws that are publicly promulgated, equally enforced, and independently adjudicated, that are consistent with international human rights norms and standards.* [U.S. State Department]

> *A principle of governance in which all persons, institutions, and entities, public and private, including the state itself, are accountable to laws that are publicly promulgated, equally enforced, and independently adjudicated that are consistent with international human rights norms and standards. It requires measures to ensure adherence to the principles of supremacy of law, equality before the law, accountability to the law, fairness in the application of the law, separation of powers, participation in decision-making, legal certainty, avoidance of arbitrariness, and procedural and legal transparency.* [United Nations]

There have been several attempts to quantify and index ROL. The committee examined and compared two of the most comprehensive efforts: The one undertaken by the World Justice Project and the other by the Varieties of Democracies Project. The committee found a high level of correlation between these two indices, and it found a strong positive correlation between a commitment to ROL and a country's human rights score as well as its level of democracy.[2] As such, the committee recognizes that future research can, in principle, assess whether police reforms can achieve outcomes with an impact on improving ROL.

---

[2] See the validation exercise in Appendix A.

The fact that such evaluations do not appear to be regularly utilized in overseas aid is no impediment to doing so in the future. Nor are the metrics currently available—including those reviewed here—the only possible way to assess reform effects on ROL. Rather, the evidence that exists today demonstrates a proof of concept for such measures in general. Improved measures can be sought to enable better evaluations of what benefits can be achieved by various strategies of police reform. Ideally, meaningful metrics can be identified for global adoption to strive for greater reliability in measuring progress within and across countries on ROL standards and protection of the public.

POLICE INSTITUTIONS AND THE RULE OF LAW

Adherence to human rights standards, understood as a set of normative commitments, is related to increased legitimacy in policing, including aspects such as minimizing the abuse of force and the provision of safety to the citizens to ensure that they can exercise their rights and obligations.

Since a fundamental component of the rule of law is that the state be held accountable to the law, and since the state delegates considerable power to the police, police institutions have great responsibility to act in ways consistent with laws and international human rights norms and standards. Promoting the rule of law therefore requires laws and policies that establish clear limits to police authority and actions—particularly regarding the use of force—as well as mechanisms for meaningful oversight and accountability. Such constraints on police authority and action to ensure they adhere to the rule of law are also important for protecting the citizenry from potential abuses by the police institution itself.

ORGANIZATIONAL STRUCTURES FOR POLICING

Organizational structures for policing have been defined as the arrangements of responsibilities and authority invested in a policing agency to include appropriate oversight mechanisms. At this date, there is no strong scientific evidence that any single form of organization is more effective than any others in promoting ROL and public protection. Given their potential relevance to ROL, the committee examined the research base for the militarization of police, governance structures, and mechanisms for handling police misconduct.

Contemporary democracies tend to maintain a separation between the roles of police (public safety) and those of the military (national security). However, this separation between civilian police and military forces has become increasingly blurred within many countries, notably in Latin America and parts of Africa. This boundary blurring is in part due to the increased militarization of the police. Despite some perceptions of the effectiveness of militarization in some countries, there is little empirical evidence to conclude that militarization is an improvement over civilian approaches in terms of reducing the harm associated with crime.

There are different models for external and internal governance structures for policing organizations, but no clear evidence about how well any of them support the rule of law. The concept of operational independence of police leaders from directly elected governments is said to support the rule of law by freeing police to arrest and prosecute government leaders when necessary. However, research in Latin America shows that police can become so autonomous that they are unresponsive to elected leadership. More qualitative and quantitative research is needed to understand these dynamics.

Internal governance that includes effective, independent investigative units within agencies may increase government and police legitimacy and foster public trust. Systematic evidence is available on internal governance structures, and it shows that police organizations with internal affairs or professional standards units that provide internal, independent checks and balances are better equipped to prevent corruption within the organization than those without cross-checks. An effective model of internal governance of policing entails promulgated procedural rules for all personnel actions, including appointments, assignments, promotions, and discipline. To promote the engagement of the community in implementing these checks and balances, a fair, accessible, and anonymous system for submitting complaints against police misconduct that is part of agency operations and is regularly acted upon is paramount.

POLICIES FOR PROMOTING ACCOUNTABLE POLICING

Police accountability (both to the community and to the government) encompasses a wide range of policies that try to control, manage, regulate, and hold police responsible for their mandates, including a range of expectations for performance and behavior and the specific daily tasks needed to achieve those mandates. Such policies can include systems for hiring, promotion, supervision, regular audits, disciplinary and internal investigations, community complaints, and monitoring with technologies. Police can be held accountable to ROL principles and to the fundamental mandate to protect the population. In democracies, this means that the police are held to account by—and to—the people who are embodied in these mandates. In practice, police agencies worldwide and within the same countries or states may differ significantly in their use of, and in the effectiveness of, mechanisms they employ to achieve accountability.

The current evidence base on recruitment and appointment of police does not permit country-level conclusions about what sort of staff profiles or recruitment policies explicitly promote the rule of law. Yet policies that support sustaining a police service that is representative of the community it serves, reflecting the diversity of that population, have shown the most promise in promoting police legitimacy and public confidence in a variety of contexts worldwide. Research, though limited to a few settings, has shown that recruitment policies and tactics can be developed to actively encourage the recruitment of underrepresented groups or remove structural obstacles to such recruitment.

Research suggests that new technologies can serve important roles in accountability systems—capturing, tracking, and even analyzing data in efficient ways that will help monitor policing activities. However, this depends on how these technologies are used in practice, the strength and supervision of implementation policies, and whether citizens and the police share similar expectations about those technologies. For example, body-worn cameras may be effective in collecting data on police interactions and holding officers accountable to ROL and human rights standards. However, this effectiveness relies on having community acceptance, enforcement of policies that require police to turn on and use the cameras, and policies and processes that fairly determine handling of data from cameras and any infractions and subsequent discipline.

There is a growing body of research with consistent evidence indicating that policies aimed at creating a culture of accountability, fairness, and justice *within* a police department can have a notable effect on police interaction with the community. The extent to which police extend procedural justice and fairness to members of the community is likely to depend on the extent to which procedural fairness internal to a police organization encompasses respect perceived by police in their relationship with their supervisors and fairness and inclusion in decision making.

PROACTIVE POLICING PRACTICES

Proactive policing includes any task that is initiated by a police agency for the purpose of reducing harm and detecting signs of crime. It includes a broad range of activities, from foot patrol of high-crime locations to covert surveillance of human trafficking operations. To the extent that proactive policing sets priorities for the protection of human rights and the most vulnerable members of a population, it offers a strategy for making valuable improvements to a policing strategy that is often solely based on answering calls to police (e.g., reactive policing). From domestic violence to armed robbery, proactive policing offers tactics for preventing crime, not just punishing it.

It is important to distinguish an evidence-based version of proactive policing, focused on harm reduction, from more subjective or politically driven bases of proactive policing. Targets of police actions tend to be more objective and appropriate for equal protection of all members of the public when they are derived from comprehensive analyses of the distributions of serious criminal victimization across populations rather than from intuitive selections of such targets. Conducting such analyses, however, requires a substantial information infrastructure for targeting and tracking concentrations of serious harm as well as understanding the underlying conditions that may contribute to crime and victimization.

An evidence-based approach to proactive policing also requires agencies to actively and consistently assess many of their own practices, including where and when police patrol, stop people, make arrests, prosecute suspects, and injure or kill them. Doing so requires infrastructure that allows for collecting and retrieving adequate and accurate information on crime, police activity, and citizen feedback. It also requires integrating evidence from human resources policies, including complaints and disciplinary action. This data collection and analysis should be informed by rigorous and reliable scientific knowledge about effective and lawful practices in policing; and a commitment to transparency, accountability, and responsible spending related to police activities and actions. This list sets a high standard for police agencies, and to the committee's knowledge, that list has not even been met in entirety by the majority of policing agencies in the Global North.

This research and information-gathering infrastructure is important to pursue effectively two of the most promising evidence-based strategies: problem-oriented policing for protecting the public and community-oriented policing for cultivating dialogue and police legitimacy.

Problem-oriented policing is a strategic approach to tackling *patterns* of crime, disorder, and even internal challenges in policing.[3] Research evidence has indicated across a wide range of experiments that problem-oriented policing can be a promising strategy to reduce crime and disorder. Problem solving may be particularly effective at reducing crime when police target conditions and situations at specific locations and "hot spots" where crime concentrates.

Community-oriented policing is both a philosophy of policing and an organizational practice in which people within a jurisdiction, community, or neighborhood play a more active role in co-producing public safety and holding the police accountable to community concerns. Because of its close

---

[3]Problem-oriented policing need not only address external problems of crime and disorder. Solutions to many internal challenges in policing benefit from a problem-solving, proactive approach, such as the handling of officers with high frequencies of complaints from the public.

relationship to democratic ideals (inclusion of citizen input in decision making), community-oriented policing is often directly or indirectly viewed as part of promoting ROL in democratic societies. Many practices and programs aimed at improving relationships between police and the public have been associated with community-oriented policing. In practice, even well-intentioned policing agencies and programs have several implementation challenges. Recent reviews recognize that some community-oriented policing activities, programs, or interventions have not been well defined or evaluated. For the evaluations that do exist, many are of modest methodological quality and do not measure long-term effects. This body of research finds that while crime prevention or deterrence benefits are inconsistent, some community-oriented policing programs can improve citizen satisfaction with police services (although the impacts on perceptions of police legitimacy may be weaker). Whether community-oriented policing can be implemented reliably in ways that promote ROL and public safety remains to be seen.

A RESEARCH AGENDA FOR EVIDENCE-BASED POLICING

The following recommendations promote the idea that capacity-building programs must amplify lessons learned from research. Some knowledge has already been generated and can be useful for this area of activity in U.S. foreign policy, including for programs at the Departments of State, Justice, Treasury, and Homeland Security, but there is much more to understand. To this end, "evidence partnerships" across various U.S. federal agencies, and between the United States and other countries undertaking similar activities, may be fruitful. In the committee's view, only the growth of INL's recent work in building new knowledge and reviewing existing lessons can provide sufficient clarity to fully answering the questions in our mandate and realizing the goal of translating evidence into practice.

To facilitate greater adoption of evidence-based policing practices worldwide, a registry of global policing impact studies is needed. While no such registry currently exists, such a registry could serve as a foundation for the development of both measurement methods and substantive conclusions that will advance qualitative and quantitative evidence and further inform practice. The registry should be designed to manage documents in multiple languages and extend the knowledge accumulated to researchers across countries. Further, the registry should promote the growth of research in Global South countries. Effort will need to be made to group studies by country similarities (cultural or other relevant characteristics), as this can serve to aid moderator analyses in systematic reviews.

RECOMMENDATION 1: In pursuit of better knowledge management, foreign assistance donors, including the Bureau of International Narcotics and Law Enforcement Affairs, U.S. Department of State, should support the establishment of an open, online registry of all available research worldwide on police organizational policies, structures, and practices with outcomes measuring the rule of law and public protection and analysis of contextual factors contributing to these outcomes.

Existing training programs that discuss police organizational structures, policies, and practices need to reflect the available evidence related to organizational structures, policies, and practices. Foreign assistance donors, such as INL, should examine their training in light of material and resources provided here and be prepared to continue to adapt curricula as additional new knowledge emerges.

RECOMMENDATION 2: Foreign assistance donors, including the Bureau of International Narcotics and Law Enforcement Affairs, U.S. Department of State, should conduct an evidence-based assessment of their training modules to determine how aligned the curricula are with available evidence on the outcomes of organizational structures, policies, and practices that promote the rule of law and protection of the public and on the contexts in which such structures, policies, and practices work.

The committee recognizes that there are no simple answers to guide decisions around organizational policies, structures, and practices that promote ROL and protect the population. Much organizational effectiveness depends on cultural, political, and social conditions, and such conditions can vary both between and within countries. With better contextualization, many lessons from research in other countries can be tested for applicability in new settings. It would benefit donor efforts to have a better understanding of the conditions that affect the success of organizational-level interventions.

RECOMMENDATION 3: Foreign assistance donors should encourage, and possibly commission, research that examines the cultural, political, and social conditions in which police operate—and assesses which of the contextual variables are likely to lead to successful outcomes from different kinds of police assistance efforts.

There are key gaps in the literature concerning evaluations of policing across different contexts and countries; standard measures of inputs, outputs, and effectiveness; a systematic account of underlying assumptions of such measures; and reliable counting of those measures. Such standards are needed to interpret the meaning of research results, as uncertainty over the reliability of measurement is a major impediment to translating science into practice.

Foreign assistance donors are in a position to help facilitate the development of a research framework to assess policing interventions in multiple contexts, as well as the development of police-researcher partnerships to expand available policing research and advance evidence-based policing. Local research capacity exists in many countries, even in areas of high violence and civil unrest, but may lack the funding and incentives to form police-researcher partnerships.

> RECOMMENDATION 4: To gather data and expand available policing research, foreign assistance donors, including the Bureau of International Narcotics and Law Enforcement Affairs, U.S. Department of State, should incentivize partner countries to monitor, track, and evaluate the implementation of promising approaches and other initiatives by linking resources to establish police-research partnerships in assistance agreements.

> RECOMMENDATION 5: To advance a policing research framework suitable for multiple countries, foreign assistance donors should raise awareness in host countries of the value of recording and reporting crime and harm metrics. In addition, they should encourage the research community to establish a model crime reporting system for violent crimes and the identification of geographic concentrations of harm from crime and disorder to strengthen understanding of both crime and how officers are responding to crime across countries.

1

Introduction and Overview

What evidence does the existing state of science offer to help advance global reforms in policing? In particular, what research can help guide efforts in a wide range of countries to enhance police capability to promote the rule of law and protection of the public? These questions are especially important during this critical juncture for policing around the world and are a priority of the U.S. Department of State's Bureau of International Narcotics and Law Enforcement Affairs (INL). The mission of INL is to help "partner governments assess, build, reform, and sustain competent and legitimate criminal justice systems, and [develop and implement] the architecture necessary for international drug control and cross-border law enforcement cooperation."[1] To advance its own efforts to build knowledge, assess existing evidence, and improve its programs, INL asked the Committee on Law and Justice (CLAJ) of the National Academies of Sciences, Engineering, and Medicine to convene an ad hoc consensus committee to review and assess existing evidence on policing institutions, police practices and capacities, and police legitimacy in the international context.[2]

---

[1] For more information about the Bureau, see https://www.state.gov/about-us-bureau-of-international-narcotics-and-law-enforcement-affairs.

[2] Recent legislation (The Foundations for Evidence-Based Policymaking Act of 2018) also directs federal agencies to improve the use of evidence and data to generate policies and inform programs.

THE COMMITTEE'S CHARGE

The Committee on Evidence to Advance Reform in the Global Security and Justice Sectors was assembled to identify the best available research evidence about policing that can support both the promotion of the rule of law (including human rights) and protection of the public. These two themes are defined in more detail in subsequent sections of this report. The committee comprises experts in criminology, economics, international and organized crime, law, policing, and political science, and it brings knowledge and experience from a portfolio of work that spans four continents.

Given the wide range of countries with which INL works and to which these questions might be applied—from democracies to authoritarian, corrupt, and fragile regimes that are limited in capacity or otherwise unlikely to be partners in reform—there can be a major challenge of contextual "fit." Programs that work in some countries may not work in others. The same tactics, strategies, and interventions that could be successfully used in one state may backfire in another (or even be used to oppress people or violate human rights). Further, even where research findings about high-quality policing exist, they are not routinely used across and within country contexts that have similar policing structures. It is not only a question of "what works," but "what works where" and "what works when."

The committee was asked to consider these concerns and contexts while at the same time determining the applicability of existing research knowledge in policing, some of which has been reviewed by previous CLAJ consensus committees (see National Research Council [NRC], 2004, 2005; and National Academies of Sciences, Engineering and Medicine [NASEM], 2018). The committee was charged with producing a series of five reports, each addressing questions of interest to INL (see Box 1-1). To assist with this charge, the committee developed a series of five workshops to bring together both researchers who know the current and evolving state of scientific findings and practitioners who understand the decision-making environment, to address the questions in Box 1-1.

Public Workshop

This report is the first in the series, addressing the first question in the committee's charge: *What organizational policies, structures, or practices (e.g., HR and recruiting, legal authorities, reporting lines, etc.) enable a police service to promote the rule of law and protect the population?*[3] To

---

[3] Each consensus report in this series of five reports will be released in PDF format in sequence of completion. A final, sixth report will compile the five reports into one published volume and be available through the National Academies Press (http://www.nap.edu) in PDF and hardcopy.

address the first question pertinent to this report, a workshop titled "Police Organizational Policies to Promote the Rule of Law & Protect the Population in the International Context" was held March 24–25, 2021. Workshop participants included members of the committee, representatives from INL, and international researchers and practitioners in the areas of recruitment, operational independence, and policing reform.

The workshop discussions were framed around a commissioned paper prepared by Peter Neyroud, Institute of Criminology, the University of Cambridge.[4] The paper provided a descriptive narrative of "good practices" in a range of high-, medium-, and low-income countries and across different regions of the world. It assessed the strengths and limitations of the evidence and data for these practices and made observations on the research designs as well as the data that should be collected and reported to support and sustain the future development of the rule of law in democratic countries.

The workshop examined what is known and unknown (or untested) regarding re-constructing the policing landscape across entire countries, police recruitment policies, and the impact of police operational independence. Panelists were invited from the Northern Ireland Human Rights Commission, the United Nations Police Division, and academic institutions with expertise in researching these themes and experience in executing police reforms. Discussions at the workshop were a primary source of information for the committee's deliberations, and speakers were identified based on the relevance of their work to the study question. Speakers with extensive experience internationally or in postconflict settings were prioritized to better ensure the utility of their comments to the report and sponsor. The committee met three times after the workshop to reach consensus on its conclusions and recommendations and to finalize its report. The committee was tasked with writing this report in a matter of months; the report therefore presents an overview of the state of research and highlights promising areas. It does not comprehensively describe all relevant research. This report does not provide a full proceedings of the workshop.[5] Rather, it uses selected information from these resources (found as boxes throughout the report) as a springboard for offering conclusions and research agendas for the first question in the committee's charge.

---

[4] Available on the project webpage: see https://www.nationalacademies.org/our-work/evidence-to-advance-reform-in-the-global-security-and-justice-sectors.

[5] Full recordings of the workshop are available: see https://www.nationalacademies.org/event/03-24-2021/evidence-to-advance-reform-in-the-global-security-and-justice-sectors-workshop-1-public-session-1.

BOX 1-1
Statement of Task

An ad hoc committee of the National Academies of Sciences, Engineering, and Medicine will consider evidence in the areas of policing institutions, police practices and capacities, and police legitimacy in the international context. The committee will hold a series of five public workshops; each of the workshops will focus on a targeted set of questions of interest to the State Department and serve as the primary data source for a brief consensus report. Drawing on relevant literature, particularly from the international context, the project will inform the State Department's capacity-building activities aimed at strengthening the effectiveness of local, in-country law enforcement agencies, building the technical skills of foreign law enforcement personnel through training and technical assistance, and assisting in institutional police reform at the local level.

Each of the five (5) workshops will bring together experts to discuss the evidence and its implications for the international sector, as well as practitioners using the evidence to implement policy. Some papers may be commissioned for one or more workshops. The committee will issue brief independent consensus reports after each public workshop. These reports will include conclusions and recommendations, as appropriate, and will provide practical guidance on key implications of the evidence for the field.

1. **What organizational policies, structures, or practices (e.g., HR and recruiting, legal authorities, reporting lines, etc.) enable a police service to promote the rule of law and protect the population?**
2. What are the core knowledge and skills needed for police to promote the rule of law and protect the population? What is known about mechanisms (e.g., basic and continuing education or other capacity building programs) for developing the core skills needed for police to promote the rule of law and protect the population?
3. What policies and practices for police use of force are effective in promoting the rule of law and protecting the population (including officers themselves)? What is known about effective practices for implementing those policies and practices in recruitment, training, and internal affairs?
4. What policing practices build community trust and legitimacy in countries with low-to-moderate criminal justice sector capacity?
5. What is the relationship between police agencies and forensics labs obtaining accreditation and how they conduct operations on a day-to-day basis?

The Committee's Interpretation of Its Charge

The broad questions about public protection and rule of law extend through all five workshops and consensus reports, which collectively seek to accomplish the ultimate goal of the committee's work: informing the U.S. Department of State's (hereafter, State Department) capacity-building activities aimed at (1) strengthening the effectiveness of local, in-country law enforcement agencies, (2) building the technical skills of foreign law enforcement personnel through training and technical assistance, and (3) assisting in institutional police reform at the local level.

These questions were examined in the contemporary context of the State Department's assistance to approximately 90 countries, as well as that of related foreign assistance efforts by the United Kingdom and Australia, working with the same or similar countries. INL programs focus on reforming or strengthening police effectiveness within host countries. The amount and type of assistance provided to specific police organizations and functions vary and are typically based on country-specific assessments. In some cases, INL police assistance programs may target areas for functional reform and capacity building, such as improving police training, internal accountability, police-community relations, civil disorder management and control, or management and supervision.[6] All such programs share a general proposition that assistance from the United States can contribute to sustainable, institutional development in partner countries.

However, the committee is also keenly aware that even in the Global North, the United States in particular, high-quality knowledge from research is often not applied or heeded, and challenges to effectively promoting the rule of law and protecting the public are also prevalent. For example, during this committee's deliberation, police agencies in the United States were being scrutinized for officer killings of unarmed people, excessive uses of force, corruption, and insurrectionists within their own ranks, and more generally they were being scrutinized for ineffectiveness in achieving everyday mandates.[7] By making suggestions to INL, the committee assumes that the same recommendations could benefit all police agencies more generally.

The committee considered both the magnitude of the inquiry and the limitations of the current state of knowledge in scope and application. Given its charge to draw on literature from the international context, the committee understood that it would examine findings from research conducted in

---

[6] Evidence to Advance Reform in the Global Security & Justice Sectors: Sponsor Profile for the Study Committee, see https://www.state.gov/wp-content/uploads/2019/03/222048.pdf.

[7] It is important to note that there is much variation across police agencies in the United States, and while similar concerns about policing cross state boundaries, they do not necessarily apply to all police agencies in the United States.

multiple countries. Its default position was to identify the strong evidence that exists that might inform promoting the rule of law and protection of the public as well as the limits of applying that evidence across a highly variable landscape of policing. This task demands a scientific approach, which includes defining "rule of law" and "public protection," applying evidence-based principles, drawing on appropriately validated research, understanding the units of analysis, examining the outcome measures for assessing effectiveness, and considering other factors that shape the outcomes measured.

RULE OF LAW

In the briefing paper written for the workshop, Neyroud (2021) offers a thorough discussion of the challenges in defining the rule of law (ROL). Several sources provide succinct definitions of ROL. For example, the U.S. State Department's Bureau of International Narcotics and Law Enforcement Affairs defines it as:

> A principle of governance in which all persons, institutions, and entities, public, and private, including the state itself, are accountable to [domestic] laws that are publicly promulgated, equally enforced, and independently adjudicated, that are consistent with international human rights norms and standards. (See https://www.state.gov/wp-content/uploads/2019/03/222048.pdf.)

The United Nations defines the concept as:

> A principle of governance in which all persons, institutions, and entities, public and private, including the state itself, are accountable to laws that are publicly promulgated, equally enforced, and independently adjudicated that are consistent with international human rights norms and standards. It requires measures to ensure adherence to the principles of supremacy of law, equality before the law, accountability to the law, fairness in the application of the law, separation of powers, participation in decision-making, legal certainty, avoidance of arbitrariness, and procedural and legal transparency. (See https://www.un.org/ruleoflaw/what-is-the-rule-of-law/.)

Other dimensions and detailed conditions of the ROL are available in the broad legal and philosophical literature (e.g., Bingham, 2011; O'Donnell, 2004). From a scientific perspective, the committee's primary concern is how any definition of ROL is empirically measured. Given its complexity, ROL is likely to vary in degree both across countries and within them over time. That feature has generated a range of cross-country measures for the ROL (Cheung, 2019; Rajah, 2012; Versteeg and Ginsburg, 2017), each of which tends to observe the kinds of features found in the existing codes of human rights and policing practice promoted by international agencies. (See further discussion on measuring the ROL below in the section, Opportunity: Measuring the Rule of Law.)

Human Rights and Public Protection

Both the ROL definitions cited above highlight the principle that the laws of a state, as well as their enforcement, should be "consistent with international human rights norms and standards." Adherence to human rights standards, understood as a set of normative commitments (Bottoms and Tankebe, 2017), is related to increased legitimacy in policing, including aspects such as restraining from the abuse of force and the provision of safety to the citizens to ensure they can exercise their rights and obligations. Neyroud's paper (Neyroud, 2021) suggests that the human rights compliance required by ROL definitions can be achieved by a targeted approach to policing whereby police are encouraged to direct resources and police powers to areas of concentrated crime and harm. Such an approach requires having the information, data, and analysis to identify high-harm areas. This is termed evidence-based policing and is discussed in detail below and throughout the report.

The precursors to human rights violations are best pursued through informed policing (Hagan and Haugh, 2011; Scheffer, 2011). Human rights violations are often characterized by a small number of perpetrators harming large numbers of vulnerable victims. Strategically examining these crime contexts can help direct resources toward the disproportionately few offenders and in turn protect large numbers of the population. Discussion in Neyroud's paper (2021) signals the importance of criminological attention to proportionality and how it might relate to law and legal theory. This is a novel perspective, because researchers in the fields of criminology and human rights law rarely engage one another. Nevertheless, it may be essential that these fields operate with mutual awareness and in mutually reinforcing ways.

International and regional mechanisms already exist to promote respect for and to defend human rights. The United Nations (UN) Office of the High Commissioner for Human Rights represents the world's commitment to the protection of human rights as set out in the Universal Declaration of Human Rights.[8] A number of charter-based and treaty-based bodies provide mechanisms for monitoring these rights in the UN system.[9] For example, the Universal Periodic Review is a process in which the human rights records of UN Member States are reviewed and best practices in protecting

---

[8] See https://www.ohchr.org/EN/AboutUs/Pages/WhoWeAre.aspx.
[9] See https://www.ohchr.org/EN/HRBodies/Pages/HumanRightsBodies.aspx.

human rights and addressing violations are shared. Outcome reports are prepared for each review.[10]

Regional mechanisms include human rights systems in Europe, Africa, Latin America, and other regions. For example, Latin America and the Caribbean established the Inter-American human rights system in 1948, which gave birth to the Inter-American Commission for Human Rights in 1959, followed by the American Convention of Human Rights, adopted in 1969. The latter convention founded the Inter-American Court of Human Rights, whose mandate is to promote respect for and defend human rights in the region. It fulfils this mission by deploying on-site visits to observe the general human rights situation in a country, but can also investigate specific situations, and examine complaints or petitions regarding specific cases of human rights violations.

Regular reports issued by these bodies will likely provide valuable insights to agencies providing foreign assistance, like INL. Publicly highlighting priority areas for any violations may help such agencies attain adequate levels of transparency, accountability, and respect for human rights before engaging in police strengthening activities.

Police Institutions and the Rule of Law

A fundamental component of the rule of law is that the state itself be held accountable to the law. The police institution, as the entity to which the state delegates its monopoly on the legitimate use of force and with which citizens come into direct contact, has great responsibility to act in ways consistent with laws and international human rights norms and standards. The extent to which police forces adhere to constraints on the state's coercive authority is a key indicator of the strength of rule of law in a given community or country. Promoting the rule of law therefore requires laws and policies that establish clear limits to police authority and actions—particularly regarding the use of force—as well as mechanisms for meaningful oversight and accountability. Such constraints on police officers' authority and action are also important for protecting the citizenry from potential abuses by the police themselves. When police officers or police agencies engage in conduct that falls outside the scope of the law, they not only undermine the rule of law, they also directly contravene their obligation to protect the population.[11]

Measures that seek to rein in police abuses by imposing legal checks on police coercion support the rule of law and help protect the population

---

[10]See https://www.ohchr.org/EN/HRBodies/UPR/Pages/BasicFacts.aspx.

[11]In some countries, police action outside the law can result in assaults, petty corruption, and even torture and extrajudicial executions.

from potential abuses. Examples of such measures include the disbanding of Nigeria's Special Anti-Robbery Squad, which had engaged in predatory and violent conduct against citizens; Colombia's Constitutional Court ruling limiting police repression of protests; and the Brazilian Supreme Court's oversight of lethal police operations in Rio de Janeiro. Restraints on policing, starting at the organizational level and working their way down to the individual officer, are therefore an essential tool in the promotion of the rule of law and the protection of the population. Moreover, according to one recent study in Liberia, police reforms in postconflict settings may also improve citizens' perceptions of police (Blair and Morse, 2021).

EVIDENCE-BASED POLICING

The review, assessment, translation, and application of research evidence in policing has become widely known as *evidence-based policing*. This is an approach to police practice and management that involves using scientifically derived knowledge and processes to strengthen police departments' decision making, actions, and overall agency functioning. In his 1998 "Ideas in American Policing" lecture for the Police Foundation,[12] Sherman argued that "police practices should be based on scientific evidence about what works best" (Sherman, 1998, p. 2). In particular, Sherman focused on two dimensions of a research orientation in policing: (1) using the results of scientifically rigorous evaluations of law-enforcement tactics and strategies to guide decisions, and (2) generating and applying knowledge derived from an agency's analysis of its own internal issues and crime problems. Such an approach may be contrasted with policing that makes decisions based on best guesses and hunches or even personal experiences, seniority, ideologies, or feelings (Lum, 2009). The prevalence of subjective decision making in policing has contributed to the use of ineffective practices, the failure to achieve sought-after outcomes,[13] and the ongoing occurrence of preventable social harms by the police (Macbeth and Ariel, 2019; Sutherland and Mueller-Johnson, 2019).

At the core of an evidence-based policing approach is the idea that actions, tactics, programs, and technologies used by the police should actually deliver the outcomes expected of them. Sherman articulated the link between evidence-based policing and rule-of-law societies when he argued:

> No institution is more important to that success than the police, whose

---

[12]See https://www.policefoundation.org/publication/evidence-based-policing.

[13]Such desired outcomes, particularly for the aim of promoting the rule of law and protecting the public, may include improving police legitimacy and minimizing police use of excessive force, justice-related discrimination, and disparities in criminal victimization.

competence at insuring the rule of law is constantly challenged by thousands of different opinions on how police should do their job. It is therefore essential that our society constantly improves the competence of its police not merely with our opinions, but primarily with facts derived from objective knowledge (Sherman, 2011, p. 1).[14]

Evidence-based policing is also aligned with a *harm-reduction approach* to criminal justice (Chalmers, 2003; Sherman, 2013). A harm-reduction approach emphasizes that police engage in activities that reduce all harm to society, whether those harms are crimes, injuries, civil harms, or financial harms and whether they are caused by criminals, by collisions, or by oppressive, unfair, or violent criminal justice systems and their agents.

Steps Toward Evidence-Based Policing

An evidence-based approach is applicable to all international police reform efforts. To promote the rule of law and protect the population, an evidence-based policing approach requires: (1) a reliable body of knowledge about police practices; (2) the ongoing practice of evidence-based and systematic targeting, testing, and tracking in policing; and (3) the institutionalization and implementation of knowledge into police practices (Lum and Koper, 2017; Sherman, 2013).

Reliable Body of Knowledge

There exists a robust body of policing research that can inform and advise on what is known about effective police operational tactics, strategies, and internal functions. Much of this research has been conducted in the Global North and focuses on the crime-prevention functions of policing. However, a growing body of research also addresses such concerns as police efforts to improve relationships with the communities they serve; improving trust and satisfaction in specific interactions with citizens; and strengthening internal accountability mechanisms for rule-of-law policing. This body of policing research has been systematically reviewed and compiled in several publicly available resources, including two previous National Academy of Sciences ad hoc consensus committee reports (NASEM, 2018; NRC, 2004); the *Evidence-Based Policing Matrix*[15] (see also Lum and Koper, 2017); the

---

[14]From his Benjamin Franklin Medal lecture to the Royal Society for the Encouragement of Arts, Manufactures, and Commerce, London, U.K., November 2011. For the lecture text, see https://www.crim.cam.ac.uk/system/files/documents/franklinfinal2011.pdf, and for the video recording, see https://www.youtube.com/watch?v=UqOq-5udMf0.

[15]See https://cebcp.org/evidence-based-policing/the-matrix/.

Global Policing Database;[16] and the Campbell Collaboration Crime and Justice Coordinating Group's systematic reviews.[17] The development of this knowledge has required collaborations between researchers and police agencies; objective research processes and an environment in which research findings are not suppressed; transparency and openness to data sharing and research by police agencies; and adequate investment and funding in building this research knowledge.

Ongoing Targeting, Testing, and Tracking

The practice of evidence-based policing also requires agencies—including those involved in promoting policing reform, like INL—to actively and consistently assess and evaluate their own practices against consistent standards. This requires not only consistently aligning their efforts to existing knowledge about policing, but also actively testing and evaluating their own practices to determine if those practices do, in fact, achieve sought-after outcomes (Sherman, 1998). Doing that requires police infrastructure, human resources, and information technologies that allow for accurate collection of information on crime, police activity, and citizen feedback to be able to track and understand these trends. Having high-quality information on both crime and internal police functioning can then facilitate more accurate targeting of problems with solutions supported by evidence, rather than the indiscriminate implementation of vague or non-evidence-based approaches. This capacity building equally requires a commitment to transparency, accountability, and responsible spending related to police activities and actions.

In the majority of policing agencies around the world, however, those high standards have yet to be consistently met. For example, many agencies continue to regularly carry out patrol and investigative activities that are known to be ineffective in protecting the public from crime or excessive police force. Most fail to proactively evaluate their own practices for effectiveness. Many agencies in the United States do not collect comprehensive information about their officers' conduct and performance. This lack of systematic evidence undermines the capacity to create officer or agency accountability—such as infrastructures that would allow an agency to assess how well each officer is upholding the rule of law.

The absence of records or lack of transparency can create more challenges. In some countries, there is *no* written list of who has been appointed as a police officer, in turn preventing an accurate accounting of

---

[16] See https://gpd.uq.edu.au/s/gpd/page/about.
[17] See https://www.campbellcollaboration.org/contact/coordinating-groups/crime-and-justice.html.

staff numbers as well as officer fatalities. In such contexts, evidence-based policing may seem unlikely to succeed. However, raising awareness and support for the importance of record keeping and then building the capacity to create and analyze records may be precisely the place to begin a global strategy of police reform.

Institutionalization

Wherever records can be created and data generated from them, evidence-based policing can use them to implement research-backed practices. These records—with the assistance of INL or other development agencies—can inform the development and establishment of the scientific processes of targeting, testing, and tracking into the everyday systems of police organizations, including police training, supervision, management, accountability, leadership, deployment in the community, and use of technologies. Lum and Koper (2017) argue that this requires three additional activities: translation, receptivity, and institutionalization.

Translation. Research and analysis are often presented in forms that are not practitioner friendly, emphasizing scientific aspects that may be of little interest to patrol commanders working on deployment operations or community members concerned about police activities. Therefore, research needs to be translated into digestible forms, directives, policies, and tactics that are both understandable and applicable to contemporary law enforcement and community concerns.

Receptivity. Even when research is translated, an evidence-based policing approach requires that law enforcement agencies and their officers build receptivity to this knowledge, which in turn demands educational, structural, and cultural adjustments in law enforcement agencies that allow officers and agencies to be amenable to such knowledge (see specific examples in Lum and Koper, 2017). That is, evidence-based policing requires an environment open to change.

Institutionalization. Embedding research into practice, in turn, requires fundamental adjustments to an organization's systems of (and infrastructure for) incentives, accountability, deployment, supervision, management, leadership, technology, and professional development so that the organization can sustain an evidence-based approach over time (see specific examples in Lum and Koper, 2017). Evidence-based policing may also require legal frameworks and requirements to incentivize and institutionalize this approach. In theory, INL's efforts fall under this translational and institutionalization part of evidence-based policing, although INL could also be actively involved in generating evidence as well as tracking and testing.

Challenges: Social, Cultural, and Political Factors

A key question for evidence-based policing reforms, then, is what political-social conditions afford the best opportunities to use scientific knowledge and generate and apply such knowledge. Police reforms, and any associated technical assistance and training, can often be challenged by social, cultural, and political factors. (See identified challenges from the *INL Guide to Police Assistance* in Box 1-2.) Given the variations in policing history, as well as in legal systems and regime types, the starting point for police reform is likely to vary greatly from one country to the next, and perhaps between regions within a country. Resistance to the rule of law by any elements of national governance that would lose power or money can

---

BOX 1-2
Challenges to Police Assistance

INL police assistance programs can be implemented in a wide range of environments, including fragile states, emerging democracies, steady states, or in post-conflict settings. … Decisions regarding the type of police assistance program to be offered to a host nation are dependent upon a number of factors, including U.S. policy goals, the INL Functional Bureau Strategy, the Integrated Country Strategy, the absorptive capacity of the host nation, political support, and budget considerations. Ultimately policymakers and the U.S. Embassy decide the scope of INL programs. … The Leahy Law, established by the Foreign Assistance Act of 1961, as amended, requires human rights vetting. … The law prohibits assistance to any unit of a foreign country's security forces that has been determined, on the basis of credible information, to have committed gross violations of human rights until and unless the country has taken effective steps to bring responsible members to justice. …

Over the years, challenges have been encountered in connection with efforts to provide police foreign assistance….

- Resistance to Change
- Ineffective Organizational Management
- Reactive Rather than Proactive Policing
- Dual or Multiple-Level Entry into Police Service
- Existence of Public Corruption
- Absence of Police Accountability
- Host Nation Resource Allocation Favors Military
- Human Rights Abuses
- [Underrepresentation] of Women in Policing
- Poor Coordination Within Criminal Justice System.

SOURCE: Excerpted from *INL Guide to Police Assistance* (pp. 12–16, 23–24), https://2009-2017.state.gov/documents/organization/263419.pdf.

derail policing reforms, even when the knowledge and skills are ready to deploy. In some places, that resistance can be violent, with attacks on police stations and the murdering of police who endeavor to achieve reform. In other settings, resistance can be less visible but equally powerful. In addition to political resistance, social and cultural histories can shape the level of receptivity to reform. For example, the conditions under which slavery (or apartheid) was abolished likely influence the cultural landscape for police reform and may set countries apart in the ways in which they should approach reform.

Social factors, such as corruption, also impact the possibility of reform. Corruption and informal practices—both internal and external to the police organization—may have more sway over formal policies, structures, or practices and can fundamentally alter how police organizations function. Related conditions—such as when police are barely paid or resourced, where police work with directives that include political repression, or where there is overlap between police and political elites and organized crime—greatly affect what can be achieved (for example, see Gerber and Mendelson, 2008).

Examples from reform efforts in Africa demonstrate these contexts. For example, Hills (2020, p. 1546) describes Somali policing as "reflecting a series of social and political influences and relationships within fields of power characterized by inequality, with the emphasis on coercion, exploitation and accommodation." Such characteristics might suggest that donors supporting policing reform should invest in providing the minimal requirements for state-based policing to address the challenges of stabilization and development, such as context-specific vetting, basic training courses, stipends for officers, and the use of activities and buildings to signal presence.

While it can be daunting to consider such challenges, initiatives can work well when they are customized to a context, and donors can play a catalytic role. The idea of "barrier mapping," from the organizational change management literature (Lewin, 1951), may provide a path forward, as it allows planners to think about bypassing some barriers rather than confronting them directly. Such mapping, in the policing context, would consider how imported ideas may be received by local law enforcement and political elites, and how such ideas may be transformed once filtered through local interests and dispositions as well as the political will necessary to ensure not only that knowledge is accepted but that it is also effectively implemented (Hills, 2012).

In any case, identifying the barriers to change should be a part of every evaluation of efforts to reform.[18] Once those barriers are identified,

---

[18] "Pre-mortem" examinations of reform plans are similar and aim to generate ideas to consider and then avoid results on the back end, causing reform efforts to have failed (Kahneman, 2011).

along with the relevant actors, incentives, and resources, this can illuminate where and when it is feasible to proceed, where it is best not to proceed, and where it may be feasible to proceed but only with a plan for evading or overcoming any obstacles.

Challenges: Research and Measurement Issues

A fundamental question and challenge for implementing an evidence-based approach for INL's reform efforts is how progress can be measured. There are questions about what kinds of data to collect, what units of analysis to use,[19] how to manage data, and how comparisons should be made. It is important to recognize that not all police agencies are nationally governed, so country-level data may obscure the information being sought. There are many possible measures of citizen security and the rule of law, and many measures that extend beyond traditional crime statistics and measures for police use of deadly force. Presently, there is a lack of consensus over how the success of police reforms can best be measured. Even methods of counting homicides vary widely across countries (Andersson and Kazemian, 2018), as do measures of less extreme dimensions of citizen safety. Because the rendering of INL assistance can vary so widely across countries, it may not be necessary for a single measurement system of reform effectiveness to be used across them all. What may be most useful in each country is country-specific indicators. However, if a set of globally reliable measures could be developed to pass some global tests of reliability principles, there would be far greater benefits for guiding police development. Whether reliable measurement across countries and within them over time becomes more likely by improving existing measures (see discussion below) or by developing new ones is a question that an expanded research agenda for global police reform can address (see further discussion of the research agenda in Chapter 5).

Opportunity: Measuring the Rule of Law

Given the multifaceted and complex nature of the concept of the ROL, it is difficult to measure a country's commitment to it and, more specifically and relevant to the committee's charge, to measure a police service's

---

[19]In the context of providing foreign assistance, it seems reasonable to use the state (country) as the unit of analysis for measuring success or progress in police reforms. However, the disadvantage of using the state as a unit of analysis is that it limits the statistical power for measuring outcomes. There may also be advantages to using the police force itself as the unit of analysis, and in many countries those police forces exist at the subnational level. Where the police forces are administered subnationally (e.g., in Brazil, Argentina, and Mexico), there is a clear substantive and methodological reason for the police force to be the unit of analysis.

commitment to it. Notwithstanding this challenge, there have been several attempts to quantify and index ROL (Cheung, 2019; Rajah, 2012; Versteeg and Ginsburg, 2017). For example, beyond the two discussed here and in Appendix A, both the World Bank[20] and the United Nations[21] have projects to develop governance and ROL indicators. This section discusses and compares two of the most comprehensive indices which use different methodologies and sources of data to rank countries: (1) The World Justice Project (WJP)[22] and (2) the Varieties of Democracies (V-DEM) Project.[23] Both projects provide a composite ROL Index through a multidimensional set of outcome indicators, each of which reflects a particular aspect of this complex concept. The two measures are highly correlated. A comparison of these two indices is available in Appendix A.

The evidence reviewed by the committee suggests that research can, in principle, measure whether police reforms can support basic tenets of and potentially improve ROL. The committee identified candidate measures that satisfy requirements of basic face validity and are regularly produced for multiple countries over multiple years. The fact that such evaluations do not appear to be a part of current practice in overseas aid is no impediment to doing so in the future. Nor are the metrics currently available—including those reviewed here—the only possible way to assess reform effects on ROL. Rather, the evidence today demonstrates a proof of concept for such measures in general. Improved measures can and should be sought to enable evaluations of the benefits achieved by various strategies of police reform.

It is also possible to measure ROL below the country level. For more populous or sharply divided states, it may be essential to deploy surveys or other measures at a subnational level to measure, for example, the number of people who are killed by the police. With the growth in internet publication of local newspapers, it may even be possible to construct web-crawling tools to collect such data. Several newspapers have done this for tracking incidents involving U.S. police, for example, without incurring substantial costs.[24] Nongovernmental organizations can also be commissioned to run observatories to document cases of police abuse, such as the Lethal Force Monitor in Latin America (Bergmann et al., 2019) and Campaign Zero in the United States.[25]

---

[20] See https://info.worldbank.org/governance/wgi.
[21] See https://www.un.org/en/events/peacekeepersday/2011/publications/un_rule_of_law_indicators.pdf.
[22] See https://worldjusticeproject.org/our-work/research-and-data/wjp-rule-law-index-2020.
[23] See https://www.v-dem.net/en.
[24] See, e.g., https://www.washingtonpost.com/graphics/investigations/police-shootings-database.
[25] See https://mappingpoliceviolence.org.

The World Justice Project.[26] Covering 128 countries from 2012 to 2020, the WJP's ROL Index provides scores and rankings based on eight factors: (1) constraints on government powers, (2) absence of corruption, (3) open government, (4) fundamental rights, (5) order and security, (6) regulatory enforcement, (7) civil justice, and (8) criminal justice. In constructing the Index, the WPJ relies on national surveys of more than 130,000 households and 4,000 legal practitioners and experts. These primary sources are used to measure how the rule of law is experienced and perceived.

The WJP defines the rule of law as a durable system of laws, institutions, norms, and community commitment that delivers (1) accountability (the government, as well as private actors, are accountable under the law); (2) just laws (the laws are clear, publicized, and stable; are applied evenly; and protect fundamental rights, including the security of persons and contract, property, and human rights); (3) open government (the processes by which the laws are enacted, administered, and enforced are accessible, fair, and efficient); and (4) accessible and impartial dispute resolution (justice is delivered timely by competent, ethical, and independent representatives and neutrals who are accessible, have adequate resources, and reflect the makeup of the communities they serve). The four universal principles are operationalized using the eight factors listed above.

The Varieties of Democracies Project.[27] V-DEM defines the ROL as "the extent to which laws are transparently, independently, predictably, impartially, and equally enforced, and the extent to which the actions of government officials comply with the law." Methodologically, V-DEM's measures are based on more than 3,000 country experts who provide their judgment on different concepts and cases. According to V-DEM, they typically gather data from five experts for each observation.

The index is formed by taking the point estimates from a Bayesian factor analysis model of the following 15 indicators: (1) compliance with high court; (2) compliance with judiciary; (3) high court independence; (4) lower court independence; (5) executive respects constitution; (6) rigorous and impartial public administration; (7) transparent laws with predictable enforcement, (8) access to justice for men; (9) access to justice for women; (10) judicial accountability; (11) judicial corruption decision; (12) public-sector corrupt exchanges; (13) public-sector theft; (14) executive bribery

---

[26] The following is a snapshot of information on the World Justice Project and its ROL Index; for reference and additional information, see https://worldjusticeproject.org/our-work/research-and-data/wjp-rule-law-index-2020.

[27] The following is a snapshot of information on the Varieties of Democracies Project and its ROL Index; for reference and additional information, see https://www.v-dem.net/en.

and corrupt exchanges; and (15) executive embezzlement and theft. The measure is, therefore, a composite interval scale, from low to high (0–1).

One of the advantages of using V-DEM's Rule of Law Index is its large spatial coverage relative to the WJP (179 countries compared to 128 countries in WJP data) and temporal coverage (from the year 1789 to 2020). The V-DEM measure is less focused on street crime and public safety; many of the indicators in the V-DEM survey reflect specific components of indicators in the WJP indices. However, there are no explicit questions in the V-DEM survey distinguishing civil from criminal justice, or order and security. In contrast, the WJP survey does not explicitly ask about gendered rights or white-collar crime by government and private officials, and it does not distinguish between higher and lower courts. The analysis included in Appendix A compares these two indices in greater detail, reflecting the wide variety of ROL rankings, particularly in countries where INL operates.

ORGANIZATION OF THE REPORT

Following this introduction, Chapter 2 outlines the structures and governance within policing organizations, summarizing the various ways policing institutions are organized and the role that structures play in supporting the ability of policing to promote the rule of law and protect the population. Chapter 3 looks at the types of internal and external policies that promote accountability within policing agencies (to include internal recruitment and retention, reporting and supervision, disciplinary action, and technology). Chapter 4 examines practices of evidence-based, proactive policing, notably those related to problem-oriented policing, community-oriented policing, and the use of discretion to reduce harm. Chapter 5 lays out the committee's conclusions and recommendations.

While findings in this report provide guidance on organizational structures, policies, and practices that should be considered to enable a police service to promote the rule of law and protect the population, the report also serves as a call to researchers and funding agencies to advance the research necessary to inform U.S. foreign assistance and the capacity building of criminal justice systems and police organizations in developing countries of need. Appendix A offers a validation exercise of two ROL correlates, and Appendix B provides biographical sketches of committee members and study staff.

2

Organizational Structures for Policing

Police institutions in different countries are structured in a variety of ways, with different remits of responsibility and directives, typically informed by the government and realized by police leadership, regarding how they engage with their community. For the purpose of this report, police structures have been defined as the arrangements of responsibilities and authority invested in a policing agency to include appropriate oversight mechanisms. The previous chapter introduced the committee's endorsement of an evidence-based approach to policing, as well as defining the rule of law (ROL) and protection of the public, with an overview of existing metrics and tools used to measure both concepts. Here we focus on the question, "what organizational structures enable a police service to promote the ROL and protect the population?"

The discussion here affirms that of Bayley (2006) and Neyroud (2021); there is no evidence that any single form of organization is more effective than any other in promoting the ROL and public protection. The effort invested in reorganizing police agencies, as many Global North nations have done in recent years, offers no clear link to any changes in policing outputs or outcomes. Nevertheless, there are certain features of police agencies in some countries that attract the support of experienced observers, including the discussants in our workshop. There are also major issues in organizational patterns in Global South countries, largely concerning the relationships between responsibilities and authority of military institutions in relation to policing tasks.

The distinction between a militarized and a civilian policing service will be investigated next, followed by an examination of governance structures for policing agencies, which are theoretically linked to supporting the ROL and protecting the population. Finally, the chapter concludes with consideration of the ways in which police misconduct is investigated to ensure that improper and/or suspect behavior by police officers is counted and addressed.

MILITARY VS. CIVILIAN FORCES

As Neyroud (2021) observes, contemporary democracies tend to separate the roles of police, devoted to public safety, and the military, devoted to national security. This distinction is a central element in civil-military relations that is conducive to civilian control over the military (Dammert and Bailey, 2005). In theory, civilian control over the military is important to help consolidate democracy, reduce the threat of a coup d'état, and assert the primacy of the ROL over the rule of might.

The separation between civilian police and military forces, however, has become increasingly blurred across many countries, especially those in Latin America and in parts of Africa (González, 2020). This boundary blurring is in part due to the increased *militarization of the police*. Flores-Macías and Zarkin (2020) define militarization as the processes by which police agencies adopt the weapons, organizational structure, and training typical of the military forces. The boundary is further eroded in countries where soldiers are increasingly replacing civilian police in policing tasks. Flores-Macías and Zarkin (2020) refer to this latter process, by which armed forces take on the responsibilities of civilian police agencies, as the *constabularization of the military*.

At the committee's public workshop, Gustavo Flores-Macías described a continuum of militarization, which extends from nonmilitarized police to the constabularization of the military. There can be varying levels of militarization within countries, as the organizational structure of policing shifts from low degrees of centralization and hierarchy to higher degrees of centralization and hierarchy. Training may also shift from a focus on maintaining public order with minimal and nonlethal use of force to one focused on establishing order through specific tactical formations with stronger use of force in challenging environments. According to Flores-Macías, these variations in organizational structures influence the physical and psychological distance between police and the population. In Latin America, this distance is widening, and it is viewed as contributing to police indifference to escalating conflict and human rights violations (see Box 2-1 for additional information on the militarization of the police in Latin America).

BOX 2-1
Militarization of Law Enforcement in Latin America (Workshop Presentation)

At the workshop, Gustavo Flores-Macías, Cornell University, shared his research on the militarization of law enforcement in Latin America. In this context, civilian police departments have struggled for decades to contain rising violent crime. A combination of state weakness and electoral incentives is leading politicians to react to complex public safety problems by deploying the armed forces. Some countries, such as Honduras, have embraced militarization, with the armed forces taking the lead in antidrug efforts. Flores-Macías believes another driver is U.S. foreign policy, as large amounts of foreign aid have been prioritized toward the militarization of law enforcement in the region—more than what is directed toward strengthening civilian institutions.

Flores-Macías shared public opinion data that demonstrated public support for militarization in Latin America (Flores-Macías and Zarkin, 2022). In 2014, countries that had the most violent crime, such as El Salvador and Honduras, had the highest public support for armed forces; 86 percent and 83.7 percent respectively. But even in other countries where violent crime was not as high, such as Chile and Uruguay, support for the armed forces fighting crime was reported to be more than 50 percent. In a recent experiment, respondents in Mexico were shown images of the same people wearing different uniforms (one military and the other police) and asked about their perceptions regarding law enforcement effectiveness, respect for human rights, and propensity for corruption; on these matters, respondents rated those in military uniforms more positively than those in police uniforms (Flores-Macías and Zarkin, 2022).

Flores-Macías presented the results of a study of homicides and kidnapping in Mexico and found that such violence increased dramatically following militarization (Flores-Macías, 2018). Similarly, studies have found a rise in human rights violations following the introduction of security forces in 2006 (Flores-Macías and Zarkin, 2020). He also noted that militarization diverts resources away from the police and civil institutions. In Latin America, he said, militarization has contributed to the criminalization of poverty. Flores-Macías recognized a high correlation between low-income levels and underrepresented minorities in the region. He expressed concern about the threats to the quality of democracy in the region and the contributions that militarization is making to higher levels of violence.

Flores-Macías acknowledged that this type of research is challenging. Some of the research is experimental, while other studies are observational. Different types of law enforcement can coexist at one time, making it difficult to isolate certain features outside of purely civilian police or military presence. He added that the military assignments to certain geographical units are not random, but most often operate in the more challenging environments and regions.

NOTE: This speaker summary is presented as a factual accounting of what was presented at the workshop for the committee's consideration. The statements reflected here are those of the individual presenter and do not necessarily represent the views of all workshop participants or the committee.

Militarization of Police

One aspect of the militarization of police entails providing policing organizations with military-grade equipment. The evidence on the effects of such equipment is mixed and inconclusive. In the United States, a small number of studies have examined the impact of low-cost transfers of surplus military equipment (ranging from computers to armored vehicles) to police departments through the federal 1033 program. Bove and Gavrilova (2017), Harris and colleagues (2017), and Masera (2021) all find that violent crime fell when departments received equipment via the 1033 program, using data on equipment availability (the proximity of a county to an army distribution center) and shifting expenditures as well as crime reports and citizen complaints. However, these findings are contested; Gunderson and colleagues (2021) identify inaccuracies in the 1033 data used in Bove and Gavrilova (2017) and Harris and colleagues (2017), and find that correcting these errors, and disaggregating the unit of observation, attenuates both the magnitude and statistical precision of their estimates. Evidence on the impact of the 1033 program on police violence against citizens and community satisfaction is even more uncertain: Bove and Gavrilova (2017) and Harris and colleagues (2017) find little change, but Masera (2019) finds an increase in both killings by police and assaults against police officers. Lowande (2021) identifies no change in reported violent crime after the 1033 program was terminated and much of the acquired military equipment was returned.

In addition to issues of measurement and aggregation, none of these studies is able to estimate the "first stage impact" of these transfers on the actual use of military-style equipment by the department; the methods are limited to what economists call "reduced form" analyses, without a clear measure of exactly how much the 1033 program actually increased police militarization. Stronger conclusions would require a measure of the amount of military-grade equipment used by different agencies, data that are not regularly collected, in order to determine the extent to which the 1033 program increased militarization, or simply crowded out the purchase of military-grade gear that would have occurred anyway.

Another aspect of the militarization of police concerns the use of military-style force units (e.g., SWAT teams). Mummolo (2018) compares crime and officer safety across departments that mobilize military-style force (SWAT teams) more or less often, and finds that departments that frequently deploy SWAT teams work in areas with higher crime rates and more violence against officers. The policy interpretation of this correlation is unclear.

Constabularization of the Military

The nascent literature on the constabularization of the military focuses on two related questions: (1) What factors contribute to the constabularization of the military? and (2) What is the effect of constabularization on crime and violence as well as on the ROL more generally (including human rights, democratic stability, and legal order)? Is there evidence that the military is more (or less) effective than the police in enhancing public safety? The committee finds the evidence on these questions to be inconclusive.

Two key factors are commonly cited as an impetus for constabularization. One is increased insecurity due to dramatic increases in gang-related violence. In Latin America, this is tied to the war on drugs and governmental crackdowns on ungoverned spaces such as *favelas* (e.g., Dell, 2015). The second driver is theorized as the popularity of constabularization with the public. Public opinion supporting use of the military for police tasks has been tied to low esteem for police in many developing countries. Studies analyzing public opinion data from the Latinobarómetro and the Afrobarometer show high levels of citizen distrust in the civilian police force "to do its job in a successful, transparent, and humane manner" (p. 5). Police are often viewed as "inept, corrupt, outnumbered, and outgunned by lethal criminal syndicates with sufficient resources to purchase police docility or connivance" (Pion-Berlin and Carreras, 2017, p. 7). At the same time, popular trust in the armed forces is both high in absolute terms and much higher than trust in civilian police forces. Indeed, Pion-Berlin and Carreras (2017) find that citizens' support and requests for military crime fighting becomes higher when satisfaction with the police declines. Yet while popular support for a particular type of policing is an important component of the ROL, systems of majority rule do not necessarily contain safeguards against the exploitation or persecution of minority groups.

There is ongoing debate about the effect of constabularization on crime and violence and its relative effectiveness compared to outcomes from civilian police operations. Advocates view constabularization as necessary if temporary measures to curb rampant crime, especially given the militarization of organized crime (Pion-Berlin and Carreras, 2017). By contrast, critics argue that by using excessive force, constabularization causes an increase in violence and human rights violations (Flores-Macías and Zarkin, 2019) without necessarily deterring or incapacitating criminals (Muggah et al., 2018). Constabularization can also be used as a political strategy. In 2010, the South African Police Service engaged military ranks and established a rhetoric of force, in order to portray an anticorruption image that would appeal to the public's desire for protection and retribution (Faull, 2010).

Unfortunately, much of the debate is anecdotal (see critique by Blair and Weintraub, 2021), with arguments generally based on trends in crime—for example on rising or falling homicide rates before and after constabularization policies are implemented (Muggah et al., 2018)—that may not capture underlying causal processes, and may in fact obscure them. For example, if the military is sent to the hardest places to police, or where the level of violence is already trending upwards, then a positive association between constabularization and measures like homicide may simply reflect outcomes of other causes.

Among the handful of studies paying closer attention to causal identification, there is some evidence that constabularization in a fight against highly organized drug cartels has led to *increase*s in levels of violence. By comparing places where the military was constabularized to other places with similar pre-trends in homicide rates, based on either a simple or weighted mean of homicide rates over time, Flores-Macías (2018) finds that constabularization in Mexico led to violence escalation relative to the proposed counterfactual places. Similarly, employing a matching estimation, Espinosa and Rubin (2015) find that military interventions in the Mexican drug war led to an increase in the average homicide rate. The committee notes, however, that the estimated effect in these studies reflects the impact of constabularization as part of an escalation of conflict between the national government and powerful drug cartels. It is unclear whether the effects estimated in these studies are generalizable beyond that specific context, namely where constabularization is part of a crackdown on highly organized and violent drug cartels.

On the other hand, there is suggestive evidence that using military forces to patrol the streets reduces crime. In a randomized controlled trial (or Level 5 on the Maryland Scale) conducted in collaboration with the Cali municipal government in Colombia and colleagues (2020) find that using military forces to patrol the streets reduced crime, but only on days and at times when soldiers were physically present on the streets. Crime rates remained unchanged when soldiers were not physically present, thereby failing to generate the "residual deterrence" effects of civilian policing, as reported by Sherman (1990) and his colleagues (Barnes et al., 2020; Koper, 1995). Despite these small or null effects of military patrols on crime, Blair and Weintraub (2020) find evidence that the militarized policing program stimulated public demand for more aggressive military involvement in policing.

In sum, much more work is needed to fully understand the tradeoffs involved in using military forces for police activities. Of note, much of the research has focused on the outcomes of militarization, that is, on the increase or decrease in levels of crime and violence; there has been very little research on the impact of militarization on the organizational structures, policies, and practices of policing.

The body of research presents mixed findings regarding the role a militarized police service plays in protecting the population and raises concerns about the consequences for the ROL. Militarization in the Mexican police has been associated with greater homicidal violence and human rights violations, but further study is needed to see if these findings hold outside the Mexican context. Studies in the United States on the militarization of police (whether through transfer of military-grade weapons or SWAT-style teams) have not consistently found crime reductions in the areas where this has been deployed. In a randomized controlled trial in Cali, Colombia, found that crime went down in the areas patrolled by the military. Notably, researchers in Colombia and Mexico have found that militarization appears to enjoy considerable public support. However, additional research is required to determine if a militarized police force has a positive impact in promoting the ROL and protecting the population.

GOVERNANCE OF POLICE

External Governance and Regulation of Police

The qualitative evidence on systems of police governance suggests that their effectiveness strongly depends on the national form of government (Neyroud, 2021). The relevant dimensions include their structures of checks and balances, as well as the location of policing under national control, local control, both forms of control, or even more layers.

Police Fragmentation and National vs. Local Governmental Control

There is considerable variation around the world in how countries have chosen to organize their police forces, including the level of government that has jurisdiction over policing (national, state, or local) and the degree of fragmentation of police forces (i.e., the number of police forces charged with providing internal security). There is no clear evidence about the effects of placing decision-making authority at higher or lower levels of government. These choices may have inherent tradeoffs as it relates to policing practices. On the one hand, commanders who are focused on smaller regions may be better able to identify and respond to highly localized "hot spots" that cause the majority of crime and disorder. On the other hand, to the extent that the actions of police in one neighborhood affect the reputation of police in other areas, particularly concerning police legitimacy, higher-level governments may be better able to internalize any costs of benefits that accrue to one neighborhood based on the decisions made in another. What difference these tradeoffs make, if any, is unknown.

Neither is there any clear evidence concerning the consequences of national or subnational organization of police forces or of the fragmentation of police forces on outcomes related to public protection or the ROL. One recent study of the organization of police forces in 110 developing countries (including 75 postconflict countries) finds that greater fragmentation of police forces can lead to increased police violence against the population and greater risk of armed conflict, though a greater *number* of local or specialized police forces had no such effect (Arriola et al., 2021). Along these lines, there is some evidence to suggest that policies that seek greater coordination and information sharing across fragmented police forces can improve police ability to protect the population. Soares and Viveiros (2017) estimate that greater coordination (through information sharing and operational coordination) of military and civil police forces in the Brazilian state of Minas Gerais resulted in a 24 percent reduction in property crime and a 13 percent reduction in violent crime, yet this finding may be primarily about numbers of people in uniforms on patrol, not about organization per se. There is little available evidence on the effects of formal consolidation of police jurisdictions, as occasionally occurs in the United States when small jurisdictions cede policing authority (as a cost-saving measure) to a more centralized government agency, typically a county sheriff or metropolitan police department. The committee is unaware of any evaluation of this type of government consolidation on aggregate crime levels, in part due to limitations on the way crime data are collected in the United States.

What does seem to matter substantially, in the view of the practitioner experts who gave evidence to the committee, is the extent to which police are operationally independent from direct political control (Neyroud, 2021; O'Connor, 2021; White, 2021). While they accepted that there is a fine balance between too little and too much police autonomy, these practitioners stressed the need for police to make decisions based on law, training, and expertise despite the transient demands of political leaders. Further detail is found in the box on operational independence. See Box 2-2.

Private vs. Public Governance

Policing scholar David Bayley defines police as "people authorized by a group to regulate interpersonal relations within the group through the application of physical force" (1985, p. 7). As this definition suggests, the function of policing is not always conducted by a public police force administered by a governmental entity. The provision of security and the maintenance of order around the world varies greatly, along a continuum ranging from public police forces and legalized private police forces to

BOX 2-2
Police Operational Independence (Workshop Presentation)

At the workshop, Sir Denis O'Connor, Institute of Criminology at the University of Cambridge, United Kingdom, defined police operational independence using the law as a reference point this way: "No politician or pressure group can tell the police what decision to make, or methods to use in a particular case or investigation." However, he explained, this independence is conditional on the rule of law (ROL) and the accountability framework, within which the police must act.

Independent discretion lies at the heart of U.K. policing because it allows for the alignment of action or use of law with the circumstances at hand, according to O'Connor. Yet how "discretion" is communicated to police officers varies quite dramatically across countries. Together, the nature of discretion, the ROL, and checks and balances provide information about the environment and the context in which operations occur. O'Connor differentiated between "thick" and "thin" versions of the ROL, saying that a thin version is to apply the law simply as it is written, but the thick version is interlocked with human rights and interlinked with good governance.

In relation to the growing prioritization of addressing harms to vulnerable populations, O'Connor noted that the checks and balances around policing are changing to reflect this, and the police, in turn, need to change as well.

There are ongoing questions around how best to measure police independence and autonomy—as well as who or what they are independent from—and how that translates into particular outcomes. O'Connor pointed out that police independence and discretion do not garner the same type of research enthusiasm as other topics, largely because of their inherent complexity.

He offered a few good reference points for reasonable accountability for decisions on independence made by police:

1. The degree of publicity and the rationale people provide for what is done in policing or when making police accountable.
2. The relevance of what process was used to make decisions, such as the consideration of evidence and facts related to population concerns.
3. The willingness to revise the process used with new evidence.

NOTE: This speaker summary is presented as a factual accounting of what was presented at the workshop for the committee's consideration. The statements reflected here are those of the individual presenter and do not necessarily represent the views of all workshop participants or the committee.

traditional or customary forces among indigenous communities and private militias with varying degrees of state authorization. In the United States, many universities and other private entities have legally constituted private police forces with considerable authority to conduct arrests and other policing duties. Meanwhile, governments often engage private militias or irregular armed groups in security provision, such as the use of private militias as auxiliary police in Afghanistan and Mexico's efforts to legalize and regulate *autodefensas* (armed vigilante groups) in the fight against drug cartels. Analysis by human rights groups and security experts suggest such experiments pose serious human rights and safety concerns[1] as well as risks for further violence.[2] Moreover, public safety provision may also involve a range of private actors, from the proliferation of private security companies (which typically do not have police powers such as the authority to arrest) to cooperation and support from the business sector.

In the United States, researchers have found that "Business Improvement Districts," which grant business groups the authority to levy taxes and administer a particular area, can lead to public safety improvements (Brooks, 2008; Cook and MacDonald, 2011). In a study of a unique program carried out in the city of New Orleans, Cheng and Long (2018) find that a privately managed police service proved effective at reducing crime "as the consequence of using more effective monitoring and incentive strategies" (p. 2). There is reason to be skeptical, however, about the extent to which such findings from the United States can be applied to many countries in the Global South. Qualitative research on security and policing in Colombian cities has shown that, depending on local context, business groups can both help to support security policies that promote protection of the population, as occurred in Medellin, and form alliances with police forces that undermine the ROL, as occurred in Cali (Moncada, 2016).

INVESTIGATING POLICE MISCONDUCT

A key structural question in policing is which agencies have the power to investigate police misconduct. Such investigations seem essential to ensure that all police activity is undertaken in a fair and impartial manner and that officers are ultimately accountable to the communities they serve. In countries with a high ROL ranking, it is generally possible for a third-party agency to be assigned to investigate potential misconduct in policing—especially criminal or corrupt misconduct. In the U.K., one police force may

---

[1] See https://www.hrw.org/report/2011/09/12/just-dont-call-it-militia/impunity-militias-and-afghan-local-police.
[2] See https://www.wilsoncenter.org/sites/default/files/media/documents/publication/horton_michoacan.pdf.

be assigned by the central government to investigate another, with arrests of even chief constables resulting from such assignments (examples from the U.K.'s implementation of police oversight bodies are explored in Box 2-3). Other models include the Central Bureau of Investigation in India, which can investigate state-run police agencies; the Bureau of Criminal Apprehension in Minnesota, which has investigated numerous police killings of citizens; and the Federal Police of Brazil, which collaborated in the

---

BOX 2-3
Police Oversight Structures (Workshop Presentation)

At the workshop, both Sir Denis O'Connor, Institute of Criminology at the University of Cambridge, and Stephen White, Northern Ireland Human Rights Commission, provided examples of police governance from the United Kingdom and Northern Ireland.

United Kingdom. O'Connor explained that the office of Her Majesty's Chief Inspector of Constabulary (HMIC) for all of England and Wales was established in 1856 to ensure the efficiency and effectiveness of local policing supported with Crown (national) funding—possibly the oldest continuously operating policing oversight body in the world. With more than 43 police forces currently under their oversight, the inspectorate (now called the HMICFRS) can demand to observe all local operations and records. Inspections can reveal whether efforts for community-oriented policing have been done well or badly, and publish the results for public scrutiny by voters. Another HMICFRS tool is its independent tracking and publishing of police practice changes and the need for them on a comparative basis. Without this knowledge, the public will have a difficult time supporting changes if they are not well explained and justified. Similarly, he noted, HMICFRS provides independent and timely evidence to enable revision in relation to harms and the highest risk legitimacy issues. HMICRFS also independently assesses the cost-effectiveness of proposed new practices compared to existing ones.

Northern Ireland. White explained Northern Ireland's policing board, which sits over the National Police Service of Northern Ireland. This board consists of political and nonpolitical representatives, including former violent extremists—even people who have been convicted of serious terrorist offenses. The chief constable is accountable to the board, and the policing plan has to be approved by the board. There are monthly performance meetings, which address contentious matters that come up. In addition, positions of local chief criminal justice inspectors, an independent police ombudsman, and an international oversight commissioner have been established to monitor the changes in the policing plan.

NOTE: This speaker summary is presented as a factual accounting of what was presented at the workshop for the committee's consideration. The statements reflected here are those of the individual presenter and do not necessarily represent the views of all workshop participants or the committee.

investigation, prosecution, and (by court sentence) imprisonment of presidents of that country.

In the United States, the elected local district attorneys in each county have the legal power to investigate the police, but may rarely do so because of the symbiotic relationships between police and prosecutors in convicting serious criminals. Because of concern about under-investigation due to this relationship, in 1972 New York State Governor Nelson Rockefeller appointed a deputy state attorney general as a special prosecutor for corruption in the New York City criminal justice system.

Sherman (1978) analyzed six years of internal investigations and intelligence on corruption before and after the appointment of the New York State special prosecutor, in order to ascertain whether there was a progressive decline in the organizational scale of ongoing corruption arrangements. Other anticorruption strategies at the same time included police internal affairs testing of officers' propensity to steal or accept bribes. Internal informants recruited at the Police Academy were also cultivated by internal affairs officers, leading to further intelligence about and prosecutions of corrupt police networks. How much of the observed reduction in organizational complexity of police corruption was due to the external prosecutor—versus other structural changes like increased proactive policing of the police—remains unknown. However, this multiagency response to public demand for more honest policing was associated with an apparent end to widespread corruption in the New York City Police Department.

In addition to internal investigations, police misconduct may be investigated under international legal standards and local independent oversight and complaint bodies.[3] These standards, which aim to promote a culture of accountability, require that members of the public must be able to report and file complaints against officers or entire agencies, either directly with the station or with the prosecutor's office or an independent investigating agency (the latter two options might be preferred to ensure lack of intimidation or harassment from the officers accused of impropriety). A fair and anonymous system for submitting complaints, the standards state, is integral to the investigation process, as without a formal complaint a formal investigation is unlikely (see footnote 3). Effective independent investigative agencies may foster public trust and increase government legitimacy by improving citizens' access to justice for crimes committed by state agents, while ensuring due process for the accused.[4] Additional mechanisms for

---

[3] See https://www.unodc.org/pdf/criminal_justice/Handbook_on_police_Accountability_Oversight_and_Integrity.pdf.

[4] See https://www.justiceinitiative.org/uploads/888326d8-77c9-4bfc-b0f2-db908fc345fe/osji-who-polices-the-police-5-7-2021.pdf.

promoting an accountable policing agency from within the organization are examined in Chapter 3.

CONCLUSION

This chapter has examined the limited evidence, primarily from case studies and the experience of police reform efforts, on whether and how organizational structures of policing agencies affect the agencies' capability to both promote the ROL and protect the population. The information in this chapter is offered as guidance for consideration in building or supporting the reform of policing structures. In the next chapter, internal policies for improving the ability of police to behave in an accountable manner will be investigated, including officer recruitment and retention, the use of technology, and internal governance.

3

Policies for Promoting Accountable Policing

Policies for police accountability encompass a wide range of principles and practices that aim to control, manage, regulate, and hold police responsible for their overarching mandates and their specific daily tasks to achieve those mandates. In modern democracies, this means that the police are held to account by—and to—the people who are embodied in these mandates. In practice, police agencies worldwide and within the same countries or states may differ significantly in the mechanisms they employ to achieve accountability, and they differ as well concerning to whom they believe themselves to be accountable. However, even in the most advanced democracies, accountability systems can be weak and undermined by other priorities. There can also be tensions between democratic accountability and police commitment to the rule of law (ROL) (Herbert, 2006). Nonetheless, the committee views accountability systems as critical to the ability of a police service to promote the ROL and protect the population.

This chapter focuses on police accountability to the principles of the ROL, as laid out in Chapter 1, and to the fundamental mandate of the police to protect the population within the confines of the ROL. The chapter explores mechanisms for police recruitment, the use of technology for tracking and monitoring police behavior and activity, and internal mechanisms for supporting a policing agency accountable to the population they serve. These mechanisms are far from inclusive of all the policies appropriate to achieve complete accountability. Here some visible issues are highlighted to illustrate the importance of critical attention to the development of policies for policing. A comprehensive review of accountability policies was not possible given the timeframe for this study.

Notably absent from the succession of policies presented in this chapter are those governing the training of recruits and continued in-service training. The next workshop and report by the committee will address issues of police training. As noted in Chapter 1, this near-future work will address these questions: "What are the core knowledge and skills needed for police to promote the ROL and protect the population? What is known about mechanisms (e.g., basic and continuing education or other capacity-building programs) for developing the core skills needed for police to promote the ROL and protect the population?"

Further, the committee recognizes that policies that govern both the police use of deadly force and tactics for managing public protests would be essential considerations in efforts to promote the ROL. Normative differences currently exist across countries in their policies, laws, and judicial decisions governing the use of deadly force. Some countries give wide discretion to police officers in deciding whether a threat to harm human life justifies taking a life to prevent that harm; others tightly restrict police discretion to kill with a web of procedures and decision frameworks that prohibit officers from deciding on their own whether to kill someone. Subsequent work and reports by the committee will address these types of policies. As noted in Chapter 1, future commissioned papers and workshops will engage discussion on two questions regarding decisions to use force and police legitimacy in relation to use of force: (1) "What policies and practices for police use of force are effective in promoting the ROL and protecting the population (including officers themselves)?" and (2) "What policing practices build community trust and legitimacy in countries with low-to-moderate criminal justice sector capacity?"

The committee recognizes that very few policies for accountable policing, and the practices embedded therein, have been subjected to rigorous evaluation. Further, studies that do examine accountability mechanisms often determine that such efforts have been poorly implemented, or that they require other factors to be effective, or that they are thwarted by the police unions or other elements of police institutions. Thus, it is premature to conclude whether specific policies strengthen or weaken the accountability of individual officers or police institutions to the ROL. In Chapter 5, we discuss how research in this area can be moved forward.

POLICE RECRUITMENT

Globally, police are increasingly serving diverse populations. A fair and open recruitment policy that promotes a workforce representative of the community it serves, and reflecting the diversity of that population, matters for two reasons.[1] First, it is intrinsically valuable for police services to reflect the demographics of the local communities they serve. They can do so through policies that actively encourage recruitment of underrepresented groups or by removing structural obstacles to such recruitment. Second, a diverse police workforce may improve police legitimacy and community confidence in the police by reducing hostility between police officers and citizens, as the case study of Northern Ireland demonstrates to some degree (a case in which its police workforce shifted from being one notably dominated by a single religion to one evenly representing the two widespread religions). This can happen through changes to the type and quality of decision making (Owens and Ba, 2021) and by fostering a sense of symbolic identification with the police. However, shaping the characteristics of police service personnel requires more than recruitment policies; it also requires a retention and promotions policy, especially for the retention or promotion of historically underrepresented identity groups. There is evidence that such groups often have negative experiences within police departments, suffering disparately higher reports of discrimination and general unfair treatment (Zempi, 2020).

In recent history, the diversification of police has particularly emphasized gender considerations in hiring practices. Promoting women's involvement in policing services and the broader security sector has been a central tenet of international reforms aimed at resolving conflicts and advancing peace processes, particularly building upon the recommendations found in the United Nations Security Council Resolution 1325.[2] The lack of women's participation in policing has had historical consequences related to procedural justice. Over the years, perceptions of procedural "injustice" have stemmed from insufficient and insensitive attention to crimes against women (e.g., rape, domestic violence). Conversely, as examined by Miller and Segal (2018) in the United States, violent crimes against women (especially domestic violence) are reported at a significantly higher rate when women's representation within policing services increases. This finding may indicate a greater willingness of the community to report the crime, or of the police to record the crime when reported (Black, 1970), rather than an increase in the crime rate itself. Meanwhile, research on the inclusion of women in police in Liberia suggests that increasing women's representation in police forces may have little effect on the police response to sexual and gender-based violence, but may increase cohesion among police (Karim et al., 2018) and increase community trust in the police (Karim, 2019).

---

[1] For additional information regarding corrupted police recruitment policies see K.R. Hope, "Police Corruption and the Security Challenge in Kenya," *African Security* 11(1), 84–108.

[2] See https://www.un.org/womenwatch/osagi/wps.

Multiple countries have explored police stations staffed by and serving only women, but with limited evidence and mixed results. In India, the opening of one such station increased the reported crimes against women by 22 percent (Amaral et al., 2021). In Brazil, the availability of a women's police station did not strongly increase in crime reporting but was associated with a reduction in the rate of homicides of women (Perova and Reynolds, 2017). Researchers in Argentina found that women's police stations in postcolonial societies improve access to justice and protect against gender-based violence (Carrington et al., 2020). The value of a women-only police station is incredibly context specific and should be explored with greater rigor across countries.

While the representation of women in police services has improved overall, their numbers are still quite limited in many countries (Prenzler and Sinclair, 2013). One workforce challenge is that disparate roles between men and women police officers exist. For example, there are policies that have created specific gendered roles for officers, directing women officers to handle only certain types of procedures and/or certain citizens. Box 3-1 provides additional information from the committee's workshop on measures that have been taken to increase women's representation in this field.

There is emerging experimental evidence on how potential police candidates respond to different recruitment strategies. See Box 3-2 for an example of randomized controlled trials replicated in multiple cities in the United States around different recruitment messaging. These studies examine whether messages that emphasize policing as a long-term, stable career option have different effects from traditional messages that focus on one's desire to serve and protect the community. The studies find that the new messages do appear to attract different and more underrepresented types of candidates.

This appeal to career stability messaging is not necessarily surprising. There is evidence that police candidates attracted by career-oriented appeals are slightly more likely to complete additional screening tests required to enter a police training academy and appear to perform equally well within the academy as candidates attracted to serving the community. Further, there is some evidence from Zambia that nurses who responded to career-oriented recruitment strategies outperform nurses responding to public service-oriented strategies;[3] such findings suggest the value of further exploring the links between motivations and performance for public service positions like the police.

---

[3] See https://www.povertyactionlab.org/evaluation/recruiting-and-motivating-community-health-workers-zambia.

> **BOX 3-1**
> **Increasing the Representation of Women in Policing (Workshop Presentation)**
>
> At the workshop, Anne Li Kringen, University of New Haven, discussed the importance of increasing the number of women in policing, particularly as their participation is currently so limited. The rate of women's participation that she observed varies across countries, from about 5 percent to 33 percent. Kringen noted that there is not yet strong evidence for why some countries have higher or lower rates of women involved in policing than others.
>
> Barrier analyses have demonstrated that multiple common processes used in hiring and training regularly exclude women from policing. For example, physical fitness requirements that prioritize upper body strength (which is typically more common in men than women) are often a barrier. Further, a number of issues have been identified in the literature related to family and maternity needs, as well as limited opportunity for advancement shaped by criteria to make promotional decisions.
>
> Kringen suggested that many qualification rules for hiring are based on untested assumptions about the relevance of certain characteristics to performing policing duties. She offered that agencies and researchers work together to demonstrate the validity of hiring criteria, implementing cross-agency comparisons when rules vary between jurisdictions, or using net scoring models in hiring where strict exclusion criteria are generally avoided.
>
> ---
>
> NOTE: This speaker summary is presented as a factual accounting of what was presented at the workshop for the committee's consideration. The statements reflected here are those of the individual presenter and do not necessarily represent the views of all workshop participants or the committee.

What would it mean for recruitment if the performance of police officers were tied to actions that promote the ROL and public protection? Currently, the United Nations recommends a vetting process that, at a minimum, excludes individuals who are "personally responsible for gross violations of human rights or serious crimes under international law" and "persons with serious integrity deficits."[4] The emphasis on personal responsibility is reflected in UN guidance, across multiple documents, to not vet candidates based on broad categories such as political affiliation or identity group. Specific actions that preclude appointment to a UN Police post include genocide, war crimes, crimes against humanity, extrajudicial

---

[4] See https://www.ohchr.org/Documents/Publications/RuleoflawVettingen.pdf.

> **BOX 3-2**
> **Recruitment Tactics to Increase Diversity of Police (Workshop Presentation)**
>
> At the workshop, Elizabeth Linos, University of California, Berkeley, presented her research on police recruitment tactics. She has worked with police departments in several countries struggling to diversify their workforce to better represent the people in the communities they serve. Her research has focused on increasing the diversity of candidates who apply to public service jobs. She found that the messages that focus on public service motivation and making a difference in the community may not resonate enough to bring new and different people into the profession.
>
> A study in Chattanooga, Tennessee, tested the impact of new messages in a sample of adults who did not have a criminal record and had registered to vote. Ten thousand people acted as the control group and another ten thousand received one of four postcards in the mail. Two of the postcards were focused either on public service or similarly on impact in the community, both with the same picture of a police officer on the front. The other two postcards were designed to test intrinsic and extrinsic motivations, respectively focusing on the challenge of being a police officer, emphasizing that the job is for someone who thrives in a difficult environment and on long-term careers, pointing out that policing is more than just a job, but a place to work for life.
>
> While the first two postcards saw no change in application rates compared to other police recruitment efforts, the intrinsic and extrinsic motivation messages translated to application rates three times higher than normal. For people of color, this level rose to four times the normal application rate. Since then, similar studies have been run with more than 20 police jurisdictions across the country. Across nearly all the jurisdictions, the public service message was the least effective for new types of applicants. Further, test scores and dropout rates for these new applicants were not statistically different from those among traditional candidates.

execution, torture and similar cruel, inhuman and degrading treatment, enforced disappearance, and slavery.[5]

These basic minimum standards for vetting police officers are intuitive and compelling. These questions also align with criminal records and background checks in the United States. In the United States in 2016, policing agencies employing more than 100 officers used an average of 14.8 different

---

[5]Other types of offenses which do not rise to these levels of internationally recognized violations of human rights are recommended to be approached on a case-by-case bases, with the following questions suggested as guidelines: (1) What was the specific nature of the abuse or misconduct and what was the context?; (2) Was it a generalized institutional practice (e.g., a generally corrupt professional milieu)?; (3) Has the act of abuse or misconduct concluded or is it continuous?; (4) If concluded, has the act been acknowledged? Has the record improved?; and (5) Has the act fundamentally affected civic trust? If so, will it be possible to regain civic trust? Under what conditions? (see pp. 21–22 of UN guide for *Rule of Law Tools for Post-conflict States, Vetting: An Operational Framework*; available at https://www.ohchr.org/Documents/Publications/RuleoflawVettingen.pdf).

Another study focused on what Linos called "stereotype threat and belonging uncertainty" in relation to written or physical assessment. This theory essentially assumes that members of a marginalized group may go into a test assuming they will not perform well, sometimes leading to anxiety, which can affect scores. People coming from a demographic group that is somehow different from the dominant group in the environment may be more sensitive to cues of not belonging. With that in mind, a study was done in Avon and Somerset in the United Kingdom, where the police department was predominantly white. The assessment itself was not changed, but the environment leading to the assessment was tweaked—in this case, the email telling people to take the test was modified. For the intervention group, language that hinted at not belonging or negative cues was removed and replaced with more positive language. This group's email said "Congratulations!" and "you've been selected to participate in the next stage," asked them to consider why they wanted to be a police constable, and said when they were ready they could access the assessment. The control e-mail read like a technical note from human resources, noting that there was no appeals process and to contact the administrator if they had questions.

The results of the U.K. study show that Black and minority ethnic candidates scored much lower (40.6%) than white candidates (58.2%) in the control group. However, the intervention group saw a large change in passing rates for Black and minority ethnic candidates (61.6%) and no change for white candidates (58.5%). While these results were exciting, Linos cautioned that more replication of this type of approach is necessary to make concrete statements about its efficacy more generally.

NOTE: This speaker summary is presented as a factual accounting of what was presented at the workshop for the committee's consideration. The statements reflected here are those of the individual presenter and do not necessarily represent the views of all workshop participants or the committee.

types of screening tools, including background investigations, credit history checks, criminal history checks, driving record checks, social media checks, personal interviews, personality inventories, polygraph exams, psychological interviews, voice stress analyzers, written aptitude tests, analytic or problem-solving ability assessments, assessments of understanding diverse cultural populations, mediation or conflict management skills assessments, drug tests, medical exams, vision tests, and fitness tests (Owens and Ba, 2021). This intensive screening may provide insight into one's character and ability to promote the ROL; however, to date, the effectiveness of these screening tools has not been successfully linked to policing performance, and they have certainly not been tested against one's ability to promote the ROL in the field (see the call for research to validate hiring criteria in Box 3-1).

There are also contextual considerations for different countries. The idea of screening police candidates for prior crimes is beyond the reach of countries without systematic crime records. Further, in some countries (e.g., South Africa), police service is one of only a few options available to low-skill individuals, and this has contributed to an extremely high number of applications for limited positions. Attention to the fairness and quality of very basic assessments of police candidates will be important in countries with limited resources and databases.

Closely related to this is the ability to track dismissals of police officers for crimes or misconduct. A system for tracking this, so that officers dismissed in one community may not be hired in other places, was only recently established in the United Kingdom and remains unadopted in most U.S. states (Sherman, 2015). Chapter 5 provides recommendations on this and other reforms that require the institutionalization of reliable digital records.

Finally, in some countries policing may not be viewed as an occupation that protects and serves the community in the first place, nor as a job that provides a living wage, but rather is viewed as an explicit tool of political elites to maintain their personal power and authority. The committee views these contexts as ones where the ROL is weak and the policing authority is not viewed as legitimate. It is unlikely that small tweaks to recruitment campaigns, as discussed here, could offset the influence of such conditions without the integration of recruitment strategies into larger reform efforts.

APPOINTMENT OF POLICE LEADERSHIP

An important aspect of police recruitment and retention is defining police leadership and its appointment. Historically, there have been three models for leadership: (1) *bottom-up*, in which all leaders are promoted from the same entry-level ranks of police service over the course of their careers; (2) *elite preparation,* in which potential senior leaders are identified as an "officer corps" at the beginning of their careers with exclusive access to promotions to senior leadership; and (3) *lateral entry,* in which high-level leaders from other contexts (e.g., military, banking) are selected for direct appointments to police leadership.

The bottom-up leadership approach is a common feature of several countries, including Australia, Canada, New Zealand, the United States, and the United Kingdom. The officer corps model is found in countries that are former British colonies, including Hong Kong, India, Pakistan, and Singapore. The direct-entry model is found in some U.S. cities, Sweden, and (recently), to a very limited extent in the United Kingdom. Recent reform efforts in Latin America have resulted in a similar approach to appointing leadership; the majority of police directors are high-ranking officers appointed by the corresponding ministers in the region, chosen from a pool of eligible individuals.

Is one model of leadership likely to be superior in regard to promoting the ROL and public protection? There are many opinions on this, but no systematic evidence. The challenge to evaluating the consequences of these models is that they are embedded in so many other cultural and political factors of different countries. Even without that challenge, changes in these systems are so rare that there is scant opportunity for even before/after comparisons, let alone controlled comparisons with control groups.

What may be more important than the system of recruitment to leadership is the training and certification required for the highest leadership ranks. This certification—the idea of *licensing* police leaders—was pioneered in the context of the up-from-bottom (constable to commissioner) systems of England and Wales. These systems require anyone appointed as a chief officer to have either graduated from the Strategic Command Course of the College of Policing (after selection from a pool of chief superintendents nominated by the 43 police forces) or to have multiple years' experience in leading police agencies in other countries of comparable size to British forces (most with a minimum of 1,000 officers each).

Once certification requirements are met, certified persons may be appointed as chief officers by local police and crime commissioners or their equivalent to fixed-term contracts of service. Once appointed, they cannot be easily dismissed. This system is intended to support operational independence, whereby chiefs and leaders who are, in theory, trained to promote the ROL are then given the freedom to exercise their judgment in support of the ROL (just as leaders of the London police were [from 1829 to 1998], all appointed to the ancient office of magistrate, a lower court judgeship). See Box 3-3 for the case of police reform in Northern Ireland and the experience leaders learned to appreciate.

USES OF TECHNOLOGY

Research suggests that several technologies may have the potential to increase police accountability to the ROL and their public safety mandates. However, achieving these outcomes depends on police services having access to essential technologies that can fulfill such mandates, how that technology is used, the strength and supervision of implementation policies concerning those technologies, and whether citizens and the police share similar expectations about those technologies. As this report recommends in Chapter 5, the most important technology for evidence-based policing is a set of digital recordkeeping systems that can track the most important facts about police, starting with a list of all police officers, reports of crime, and reports of police actions, from vehicle stops to shooting suspects.

Some of the newer technologies that may allow for additional useful data collection include information technologies, body-worn cameras,

> **BOX 3-3**
> **Case Study of Police Leadership (Workshop Presentation)**
>
> At the workshop, Stephen White, a former police leader and current member of the Northern Ireland Human Rights Commission, spoke about leadership and its influence on good policing. He called for investing in leaders—both current and future—by exposing them to other environments so they can see with their own eyes, consult with people firsthand to see what is possible, and form their own vision through experience.
>
> In the reform of policing in Northern Ireland after the 1998 peace agreement, he explained, the police had to first recognize that they were part of the social problems. It was difficult for them to think that perhaps change was needed, including more representation, more transparency, and more accountability. Learning from that experience, leaders in Northern Ireland now spend a lot of time engaging with people who have community influence, or who were former terrorists or prisoners, as well as activists involved in restorative justice in their communities.
>
> According to White, key experiences for policing leaders should include:
>
> - Engaging with the community and talking with front-line police officers;
> - Interacting with criminal justice and human rights researchers;
> - Appreciating a holistic community policing program;
> - Understanding change management, including how to plan, implement, and deliver strategic change and set principles and practices to guide what is acceptable in the process and what is not (especially important when working in global contexts); and
> - When dealing with violent extremism or insurgency, understanding the root causes and what drives terrorism.
>
> ---
>
> NOTE: This speaker summary is presented as a factual accounting of what was presented at the workshop for the committee's consideration. The statements reflected here are those of the individual presenter and do not necessarily represent the views of all workshop participants or the committee.

automatic vehicle locators, and systems for early identification of officers at risk of serious misconduct or suicide. Pressures to adopt particular technologies stem from the belief among police and citizens that technology can make policing more efficient, effective, or responsive to its mandates (Koper et al., 2014; Lum et al., 2017; Sanders and Sheptycki, 2017). For example, certain technologies are believed to improve an officer's ability to identify, detect, and monitor high-risk offenders and places, thereby improving public safety goals. Other technologies, such as body-worn or in-car cameras, officer early intervention systems (EISs), and specialized records management systems are viewed as strengthening an agency or community's ability to hold officers accountable to fair treatment of citizens, human rights protections, or adherence to the ROL. Both citizens and the police often have high expectations about what technologies can deliver and may even have incongruent expectations of what technologies should be used for and the outcomes technologies might produce. The allure of technology is also its challenge; while technologies are often seen and logically deduced as a panacea, they frequently fail to deliver the desired outcomes. They also require a significant budget for training and maintenance, which may not be feasible or prioritized in every country.

Information Technologies

Information technologies, such as computer-aided dispatch and records management systems, are accountability mechanisms meant to ensure that officers perform their duties: responding to citizen calls for service (if that is the national policing model) or recording crime reports and police actions. Such information technologies also provide data that can be analyzed to see trends in police activities and responses, which can be analyzed against expected outcomes for better evidence-based policing. Information technologies are often the least faddish, so they may be underused and undermaintained in policing without substantial efforts to gain compliance. When they are deployed properly, they can add great value to the accountability of police to their ROL and public safety mandates.

When designed well, information technologies can systematically and transparently capture, record, manage, maintain, organize, and analyze large amounts of data. They can capture crime and other public safety information as well as daily police activity and citizens' concerns and complaints about both crime and police activity. The use of such information would be necessary for an evidence-based policing approach to effectively, fairly, humanely, and transparently operate within a rule-of-law framework (see Chapters 1 and 5).

Poor information technology development can result in a police service and its community inaccurately gauging the public safety challenges it faces and failing to track what police agents are doing to address those challenges. Further, information technologies can also have unintended consequences, including making officers more reactive and inefficient by creating more reporting requirements that might slow them down or create negative officer attitudes toward all information technologies (see discussions by Chan et al., 2001; Koper et al., 2015; Sanders and Condon, 2017). The use of technology is regularly filtered through an agency's values and organizational structures (referred to as "technological frames"—see Orlikowski and Gash, 1994; Robey et al., 2000), producing outcomes that may not align with the broader ideals of promoting the ROL or protecting the population. Any decisions regarding the adoption of information technologies should consider not only how they work in principle, but also how they would work in practice in a given social context.

Body-Worn Cameras

Body-worn cameras (BWCs) are believed to generate self-awareness in officers, that is, the awareness that they are being recorded and watched, to deter wrongdoing or poor behavior (Ariel et al., 2015). As with cellphone cameras, BWCs are regarded as providing a recording of an officer's activity, especially when no other witnesses are present. Unfortunately, the promise of BWCs has yet to be realized. Recent reviews of high-quality empirical evaluation research on the impact that this technology has on most (but not all) specific outcomes have been disappointing.

As Lum and colleagues (2020) find in their meta-analysis of evaluation research, the ability for BWCs to increase police accountability with regard to their use of force and other behaviors is still unclear, despite the finding that BWCs are associated with reductions in levels of citizen complaints. Lum and colleagues (2020) conclude:

> Overall, there remains substantial uncertainty about whether BWCs can reduce officer use of force, but the variation in effects suggests there may be conditions in which BWC could be effective. BWCs also do not seem to affect other police and citizen behaviors in a consistent manner, including officers' self-initiated activities or arrest behaviors, dispatched calls for service, or assaults and resistance against police officers. BWCs can reduce the number of citizen complaints against police officers, but it is unclear whether this finding signals an improvement in the quality of police-citizen interactions or a change in reporting (p. 1).

The reason for these generally disappointing findings is not because the cameras do not work mechanically. Rather, BWCs—and police technologies generally—rely upon several other policies and practices to achieve the outcomes expected of them. BWCs may be effective in holding officers accountable to reducing their use of force, corruption, or violation of human rights. However, this effectiveness relies on agencies having and enforcing policies that require police to turn on and use the cameras. Policies must also dictate how the agency will process and actively use BWC footage for internal and criminal investigations of suspect police actions (see further discussion in Lum et al., 2020).

Automatic Vehicle Locators

Automatic vehicle locators (AVLs) are global positioning system (GPS) tracking devices on police vehicles that can determine where those cars are located at any time; other technologies include GPS on officers' personal radios or phones, which can identify where the officer is, in or out of a vehicle. This technology was initially adopted for officers' safety reasons and to locate officers quickly if they were not responding. AVLs can serve as an accountability mechanism insofar as supervisors can see where officers' vehicles are, whether officers are within the post they are assigned to, and whether they are actually responding to a call for service. AVLs do not indicate *what* officers are doing, only *where* officers are.

It is unclear how much AVLs are used as an accountability tool or whether they can effectively be leveraged to strengthen police accountability to their jobs. Jones (2018) finds that police managers and supervisors struggled with using AVL information to manage how their patrol units were being deployed and that supervisors varied widely in their use of AVL information. Nonetheless, in recent hot-spot patrol experiments in the United Kingdom (Basford et al., 2021; Bland et al., 2021), handheld GPS trackers for foot patrols were successful (after initial challenges) in delivering scheduled patrols to assigned hot spots.

Early Intervention Systems

EISs use data collected by agencies about officers, such as complaints, uses of force, and personnel data, in risk assessment tools to predict which officers may be at risk for a future harmful event, such as excessive use of force, citizen complaint, officer self-harm, or officer accident (see Shjarback, 2021; Walker and Milligan, 2005). Such systems try to identify officers early enough in their careers for prevention through remediation and correction.

The research is limited and mixed regarding whether an EIS combined with an effective intervention may be effective. After reviewing this research, Shjarback (2021) finds that simply having an EIS is not enough to reduce complaints or use of force (see also Shjarback, 2015). Worden and colleagues (2013) find that when comparing EIS-flagged officers who had participated in an intervention training to improve police-citizen interactions with those who were flagged but had not participated in that training, there were no significant differences between the two groups as to the number of complaints (although complaints went down for both groups). Others, using pre-post research designs, have found that such systems with interventions were associated with reductions in complaints (Broidy and Prenzler, 2020; Macintyre et al., 2008; Walker et al., 2001).

INTERNAL GOVERNANCE

Internal police culture may have significant consequences for external police engagement. The concept of procedural fairness internal to a police organization encompasses the level of respect perceived by police in their relationship with their supervisors, fairness and inclusion in decision making, and the values and ethos that are culturally perpetuated by supervisors (Trinkner et al., 2016).

Recent research indicates that policies aimed at creating a culture of accountability, fairness, and justice within a police department may have a notable effect on police interaction with the community. In a U.S. study undertaken in a large urban area,

> [r]esults showed that when officers were in a procedurally fair department, they were more likely to trust and feel obligated to obey their supervisors, less likely to be psychologically and emotionally distressed, and less likely to be cynical and mistrustful about the world in general and the communities they police in particular…these effects were associated with greater endorsement of democratic forms of policing…[t]aken together these results clearly support the utility of infusing procedural justice into the internal working climate as a means to improve police officer job performance … and their relationship with the communities they police (Trinkner et al., 2016, p. 3).

Likewise, a study in the mainly rural Durham, England, Police Constabulary found that identification with the organization as a result of positive procedural justice "was consistently associated with stronger motivations or self-assessed propensities across a range of desirable behaviours, including towards community policing." This study was further summarized by its authors, who said

> fairness and respect, internally within police organisations, can have a similar effect [of encouraging co-operation and compliance with the law] on the attitudes and behaviour of the workforce. Fairness at a supervisory and senior leadership level was associated with officers 'going the extra mile' without personal gain, following work rules, valuing the public, feeling empowered, and supporting ethical policing (Bradford and Quinton, 2014, p. 2; see also Bradford et al., 2014).[6]

---

[6] See also Bradford et al. (2014). For a complete discussion of the literature regarding the definitions of procedural justice, and the consequences of departments employing procedural justice, see David H.F. Tyler, "Fairness Within: Sources and Consequences of Procedural Fairness in Police Agencies," Ph.D. dissertation, Arizona State University, May 2020.

The relationship between procedural justice and positive relationships with supervisors and organizational commitment was also studied in Accra, Ghana (Tankebe, 2010); however, that study—one of the few studies in this area external to the U.K./U.S. context—did not include an evaluation of the effect that commitment had on external policing behavior. These studies have relied on the self-reporting by police officers of their perceptions and attitudes, not on objective external measurements of behavior. However, the reported results of similar studies are quite consistent in noting the correlation between police experience internal to the organization and attitudes about policing and community relations.

Internal governance structures examined in the following sections of this chapter include immediate line supervision, audits of individual officer behavior and conduct, disciplinary systems and citizen complaints, and oversight.

Supervision

Supervision in police agencies includes both first-line supervision of officers and detectives and the supervision of supervisors. First-line supervision is an essential accountability mechanism yet one that is often weak in practice. First-line supervisors are most able to see the day-to-day activities of officers, to notice problems or warning signs in officer behavior or work performance, and to directly mentor and hold officers accountable to disciplinary measures when they violate procedures. In research undertaken by Engel and Worden (2003), the perception of a supervising officer's priorities had a strong influence on whether the officers under their command prioritized or disregarded the value of independent problem solving.

In practice, first-line supervisors are rarely empowered to hold officers accountable or feel comfortable disciplining them. They might not actively supervise or monitor officer behavior and might not be aware of what officers are doing daily. These deficiencies could result from cultural impediments (including poor leadership structure and/or union concerns), lack of knowledge on how to supervise, lack of technologies, resources, or performance tools to supervise officers effectively, lack of supervision of supervisors themselves, an overwhelming or distracting workload, or even threats from colleagues. Similarly, while there may be an official "chain of command" of supervision in policing, whether each rank is similarly supervising or monitoring those below them remains unknown.

Audits

Audits can be either random or regular checkups on officer and supervisor activities and behaviors or targeted assessments and checks of specific individuals. These audits may include a supervisor or commanding officer randomly responding to a call for service an officer is handling to observe the officer's response, examining reports written by officers, examining what happened to complaints made by citizens, and conducting random quizzes for officers about their up-to-date knowledge of policies, procedures, and effective policing practices. BWC have also been used for auditing purposes, where a supervisor might review footage of police activities every so often to identify any need for corrective actions. Closed circuit televisions inside police stations could also be used in similar ways. As Neyroud's review (2021) showed, studies focused on combatting corruption by government officials have found that audits can effectively reduce corruption (see Borges et al., 2017; Olken, 2007). Audits can also be conducted at the agency level by government or civilian oversight groups and units (an example is the police inspectorate in England and Wales).

Disciplinary Systems and Complaint Investigations

Police agencies may have internal investigation and internal affairs units that may process complaints and violations of agency rules and policies. These units may review citizen complaints, carry out investigations on specific officers, and carry out audits as described above. Although rarely done in practice, they could also audit the practices of an agency more broadly with regard to disparities in service, effectiveness in activities, or extent of corruption and other negative practices (Sherman, 1978). Very little is known about the current practices of internal affairs units, even in places with well-established and professional police services. For example, in the United States there have been long-standing protective practices of law enforcement officers under investigation. Internal affairs units are often constrained by these protective practices, including police union interference, lawyers hired by officers, the invoking of officers' "Bill of Rights" or immunity protections, or officers' refusals to cooperate in investigations (Walker, 2001, 2005).

Citizen complaints in the Global North are generally handled by separate units unconnected to internal affairs investigators. Some of these are external to the police force as well, such as the Independent Office for Police Conduct in England and Wales. In most agencies in the United States, citizen complaints are investigated by police officers, but some have an independent civilian review of the investigation. An eight-city review in the United States found that complaints against officers were more likely to be sustained when a civilian review was undertaken of complaint investigations conducted by internal affairs officers than where there was no civilian review (Terrill and Ingram, 2016). Historically, these investigations have rarely found conclusive evidence for or against the factual allegations made by citizens (Reiss, 1971). Since the advent of citizen cellphone cameras and body-worn cameras, however, many citizen complaints made to internal affairs units are no longer reliant solely on an officer's or citizen's word. Whether this has changed outcomes substantially is not yet known.

Some research on organizational justice suggests that how internal affairs units do their work may also matter to their effectiveness. In an analysis of complaint data from the United States, Harris and Worden (2014, p. 1258) report that "officers who received more severe sanctions were actually more likely to obtain an additional [subsequent] sustained complaint when compared with non-sanctioned officers." They speculate that perceived unfair internal affairs practices produced this effect by creating a sense of injustice and defiance among sanctioned officers.

As recently reviewed by the Task Force on Policing for the Council of Criminal Justice (2021),[7] studies of the impacts of civilian oversight are scarce, models vary widely, and there are significant barriers that preclude civilian oversight boards from carrying out their duties. Additional information regarding ways in which police misconduct is investigated and addressed at the structural level is available in Chapter 2.

CONCLUSION

Policies, as presented here, are mechanisms for directly and indirectly ensuring that police services promote the ROL. Empirical evidence linking specific policies to the adherence of ROL outcomes is generally lacking—a theme throughout this report. Nonetheless, knowledge already gained from efforts to examine the effects of policing policies can be appreciated and help guide future research on policies that may affect the ROL and public protection. The committee finds that recruitment strategies and policies that support the appropriate use of technologies are areas ripe for investigation. Research has already begun in these areas in ways that examine the effective reduction of harm to the public, and these could be extended to incorporate ROL measures. See further discussion of targeted research in these areas in Chapter 5.

---

[7] See https://counciloncj.foleon.com/policing/assessing-the-evidence/xi-civilian-oversight.

4

Proactive Policing Practices

Proactive policing lies at the core of modern preventive policing in the Global North, especially in the English-speaking world. Foot patrol by lone officers to prevent crime through deterrence was the basic strategy of the "new police" of London that Sir Robert Peel persuaded the English Parliament to fund in 1829 (Miller, 1977). There were then no telephones with which to call the police, and no radios or automobiles for police to be assigned to respond *reactively* to calls for service; all of that had to wait for the Berkeley (California) Police Chief August Vollmer to invent and implement in 1928 (Oliver, 2017). Until then, almost all policing was proactive in determining where police would do their work—up to the point at which a citizen would summon a foot patrol officer to go elsewhere for an incident in progress.

This historical reality is relevant to thinking about the Global South, where many countries neither provide proactive patrols to deter crime nor send police reactively to manage disputes, suspicious activity, or the kinds of situations defined by police scholar Egon Bittner (1974, p. 30) as "something-that-ought-not-to-be-happening-about-which-somebody-had-better-do-something-now." The benefit that reactive, dial-a-cop policing created in relation to the perception of protecting the public seems to have been substantial, especially in providing rapid response to emergency situations. Yet reactive responses conducted using automobiles are more expensive than police working primarily in police stations, as they often do in (for example) India, until they are summoned to either put down a riot, escort a VIP, or investigate a crime that someone has reported in person in a police station—sometimes after a citizen has made a two-day walk from remote areas of the country. Dial-a-cop services are so popular in the United Kingdom that as of 2021, many police forces were promising to send police cars that would not arrive for several days due to demand outstripping supply (Rothwell, 2021).

Many, but far from all, police agencies in the Global South do supply reactive police car responses. What they do more consistently is to target high-priority suspects or criminal activities and deal with them proactively. Their proactive strategy can be carried out well or badly, as with any other kind of policing. The proactive raids on *favelas* in Rio de Janeiro led to massive killings of citizens by police (McCoy, 2021), whereas proactive patrols of hot spots in Bogota reduced property crime (Braga et al., 2019) with a minimum (if any) use of lethal force. Learning from these histories of proactive engagement with criminal activities may support the use of strategies with both greater precision and less-lethal force. A major opportunity for using an evidence-based strategy is to refine both the outputs and the outcomes of this approach.

Unlike the practice of proactive policing, the conceptual framework of proactive policing is relatively recent. Even the word "proactive" was only used in print for the first time in 1966 (Bordua and Reiss, 1966). Recent decades have seen increasing demand for policing against crimes not routinely reported to police: drunk driving, drug dealing, illicit gun sales, and human trafficking.[1] Rising discontent over such problems pointed to proactive policing as a solution. So has the identification of the small proportion of all places that suffer the majority of all violent crimes, now widely known as "hot spots" (Braga et al., 2019; Sherman et al., 1989).

Research reviews of studies that have examined the effects of *evidence-based* proactive policing strategies have shown they can have significant crime reduction benefits, especially in high-crime locations. However, there may be legitimacy costs in the overuse of proactive policing in low-crime areas (Gladwell, 2019) and attendant racial disparities in the level of police contact (National Academies of Sciences, Engineering, and Medicine [NASEM], 2018). While the intention may be to *reduce* large disparities in violent victimization rates by race (National Research Council [NRC], 1993), the overuse of traffic and pedestrian stops outside of hot spots, resulting in racial disparities in police contact, has threatened the legitimacy of evidence-based stops that would have the greatest benefits for minority groups. As with so many issues, better evidence can help improve precision, as well as create better regulation and restraint, on the very great intrusions proactive policing imposes on civic liberty.

---

[1] In the past, involving the police in such illicit activities were seen as situations which might evoke further corruption and violence (Reiss, 1971).

The strategy of proactive policing, which focuses on practices aimed at preventing crime, can be much better positioned by evidence-based policing to support human rights and public protection, as articulated in Chapter 1, as well as support procedurally fair encounters between the police and the public. See Box 4-1 for a definition of proactive policing. The dilemma is whether proactive policing promotes the rule of law since it is sometimes performed outside or beyond the law, compared to reactive policing which *may* be limited to the direct application of existing laws to reported violations. It is the committee's view that the benefits of a proactive strategy could be realized if undertaken in compliance with the rule of law and carried out through an evidence-based approach outlined in Chapter 1. Certain policing practices that have been characterized as proactive strategies (NASEM, 2018) and benefit from generating and applying knowledge in an evidence-based approach are described further in this chapter: *problem-oriented policing, community-oriented policing,* and *the use of discretion.*

PROBLEM-ORIENTED POLICING

Problem-oriented policing is a strategic approach to tackling crime, disorder, and even internal challenges in policing. This approach begins with a fundamental assumption: that no event, call for police service, or public safety incident is unique or unrelated. Instead, events are connected to each other by some underlying problem or causal mechanism. For example, one offender may be responsible for several crimes in a particular area because they live nearby and opportunities to offend occur on their way to school

---

BOX 4-1
Defining Proactive Policing

In its 2018 report *Proactive Policing: Effects on Crime and Communities,* a previous committee of the National Academies of Sciences, Engineering, and Medicine defined the term "proactive policing" as referring to all policing strategies that have as one of their goals the prevention or reduction of crime and disorder and that are not reactive in terms of focusing primarily on uncovering ongoing crime or on investigating or responding to crimes once they have occurred. Specifically, the elements of proactivity include an emphasis on prevention, mobilizing resources based on police initiative, and targeting the broader underlying forces at work that may be driving crime and disorder. This contrasts with reactive policing, which involves an emphasis on reacting to particular crime events after they have occurred, mobilizing resources based on requests coming from outside the police organization, and focusing on the particulars of a given criminal incident.

SOURCE: NASEM (2018, p. 1).

or work. Robberies may be concentrated at a particular bar because patrons carry cash to the bar and leave the establishment intoxicated and vulnerable to attack. A local grocery store may suffer from numerous thefts or fights in the afternoon, because it is located near a school, and youth may socialize at that store after school. An intersection may frequently experience car accidents because motorists cannot see a stop sign that is blocked by a tree. Gang violence may be especially deadly in certain areas if gangs have easy access to firearms or are near competing gangs. Each of these recurring events reflects an underlying reason or problem causing the resulting incidents to be reported to the police. Problem-oriented policing thereby questions a reactive, case-by-case, incident-by-incident approach to dealing with crime patterns, and instead advocates that such events reflect underlying causes that can be identified, analyzed, and addressed to reduce the reoccurrence of those patterns in the future.

First envisioned by Goldstein (1979, 1990) as a department-wide strategy, problem-oriented policing was most popularly captured as an implementation plan by Eck and Spelman's (1987) SARA model, whose acronym denotes four steps: Scanning, Analysis, Response, and Assessment. *Scanning* refers to identifying problems by, for example, noticing repetitive calls for police services to the same location, or when community members continue to notify the police of an ongoing public safety problem in their neighborhood. *Analysis* involves a systematic, detailed, and deep-dive assessment of the problem, to determine not only the nature of the problem itself, but what might be the underlying causes of that problem. Once a problem is identified and deeply analyzed, a tailored *response* is developed. From an evidence-based perspective, responses should be selected based on their ability to actually deliver on the outcome sought (which is often determined through rigorous evaluation). However, if an evidence-based approach has not yet been developed and tested, problem-oriented policing relies on developing tailored and targeted responses to increase the likelihood that the response will be effective. An evidence-based approach is built into the problem-solving SARA model through the final step of assessment. *Assessment* requires that implementation of the response is tracked and documented and that there is some attempt to reliably determine if the response mitigated the problem. In total, the SARA model thereby implies that responses would be adjusted if they are inadequate, or scanning and analysis might be repeated if needed.

Research evidence has indicated that problem-oriented policing can be a promising strategy to reduce crime and disorder. A review by the National Academies of Sciences Consensus Committee on Proactive Policing (NASEM, 2018) and a Campbell Systematic Meta-Analysis (Hinkle et al., 2020) both find that a police department's commitment to problem-solving strategies can reduce crime and disorder, when implemented well (although more rigorous experimental evaluations are needed in this area). Problem solving may be particularly effective at reducing crime, at least in the short run, when police target conditions, offenders, victims, and situations at specific locations and "hot spots" where crime concentrates (Braga and Bond, 2008; Braga and Weisburd, 2012; Taylor et al., 2011). These are often places where the routine activities of offenders and victims intersect and which have environmental features and lack of guardianship[2] that can facilitate (or block) crime (see extensive discussion of these ideas by Brantingham and Brantingham, 1993; Clarke and Felson, 1993; Eck and Weisburd, 1995; Sherman et al., 1989).

Additional problem-solving strategies that are promising in reducing crime and disorder include situational crime prevention, nuisance abatement, code enforcement, clean-up activities, abatement of physical disorder, improvement of social services, and working with place-managers to increase guardianship (for examples, see Braga and Bond, 2008; Clarke, 1997; Eck and Wartell, 1998; Mazerolle et al., 2000; Weisburd et al., 2010). Braga and Weisburd (2006) note that many problem-solving projects are often "shallow" in their implementation, focusing more on enforcement efforts rather than in-depth problem solving.

When implemented well, problem-solving approaches are also aligned with responsive, transparent, and accountable policing, which are all important requirements within effective ROL policing. Problem solving requires the accurate collection, collation, and analysis of public safety data and information, which means that police agencies must have reliable and accurate information systems that can record and collect information about crime. It also requires consistent and systematically collected citizen input not just about crime problems but also about police response to those problems to respond and assess responses accurately. This allows for an evaluation not just of the impact of a particular police action on crime, but also of the impact of such an action on community perceptions of safety overall and of the legitimacy of police at the officer and institutional level. In this way, problem-oriented policing often has community-oriented elements. Problem solving establishes the critical "feedback loop" that Sherman (1998) emphasized is a cornerstone of an evidence-based approach and that can strengthen police accountability to public safety mandates and citizen concerns.

Additionally, problem-oriented policing need not only address external problems of crime and disorder. Many internal challenges in policing also reflect a problem-solving, proactive approach. For example, early intervention systems that identify officers who are at high risk of a future adverse

---

[2] Guardianship is an enlightened function where police serve to maintain the social order and protect citizens.

event, such as a complaint, excessive use of force, corruption, or self-harm, are grounded in a problem-oriented approach. Such systems are built on the assumption that officers' individual adverse activities may be combined to predict their future risk of an adverse event and that such officers should therefore be identified for early intervention. Agencies may have systemic challenges, such as officer absenteeism, excessive use of sick leave, or officers abandoning their assigned posts while on duty. These behaviors may be indicative of problems in an agency's accountability, supervisory, or disciplinary infrastructure, or may be the result of hidden incentives for officers to not carry out their duties. These underlying problems can also be identified through a problem-solving approach (e.g., SARA). In this way, a problem-solving approach to both external and internal challenges in policing can be a promising "next practice" to strengthening an agency's ability to promote the rule of law and protect the population.

In an evidence-based policing approach, agencies need critical infrastructure elements to implement and institutionalize a problem-solving approach in a consistent and meaningful way. As Lum and Koper (2017) discuss, these elements include having information technologies, analysts, and strong two-way communication channels between the police and the community to regularly collect, scan, and identify challenges within the community. However, even low-resource police agencies can adopt a problem-solving approach in the absence of information technology and analytic infrastructure by prioritizing the use of basic problem-solving skills to address chronic problems.

To implement a problem-solving approach, patrol deployment models would have to prioritize proactive problem solving rather than just reactive response to calls for service, and doing so would require adjustments to how officers are deployed and how officers and first-line supervisors are trained. An accountability infrastructure to record, document, and help assess problem-solving efforts would also need to be developed and built into the police agency's rewards, incentives, and disciplinary subsystems. As with evidence-based policing and other reforms, agency personnel across the ranks would need to subscribe to this policing approach and understand that the mandates of policing are not simply to respond and react, but to proactively problem solve to prevent. Problem-solving tactics and activities would also need to be monitored to ensure that they are not inadvertently harming the community, such as causing greater disparities or inequities in the justice system or leading to greater police violence or uses of force.

Perhaps the greatest challenge that evidence-based policing confronts is the first of the "Three T"s of targeting, testing, and tracking (Sherman, 2013). The scanning component of the SARA model, which roughly corresponds to the "targeting" element of evidence-based policing, has long been susceptible to subjectivity in selecting which patterns to prioritize. An evidence-based perspective has recently helped to combat subjective targeting through the use of a crime harm index, an approach that has spread from Canada to the United Kingdom, Australia (House and Neyroud, 2018), Denmark (Andersen and Mueller-Johnson, 2018), Sweden (Kärrholm et al., 2020), New Zealand, and Uruguay (Weinborn et al., 2017). Any form of a consistent harm weighting for each offense type provides a far more objective and systematic basis for choosing *which* crime or harm patterns to prioritize, in terms of the greatest public benefit for the investment of police resources in prevention. Adding a measurement of total crime harm value to the design of a proactive problem-oriented plan to reduce that harm holds substantial potential for increasing the fairness, legitimacy, and impact of the approach.

COMMUNITY-ORIENTED POLICING

Community-oriented policing is both a philosophy of policing and an organizational strategy (Greene, 2000; NRC, 2004) in which people within a jurisdiction, community, or neighborhood play a more active role in "co-producing" public safety and holding the police accountable to community concerns (see definitional discussions by Eck and Rosenbaum, 1994; Green and Mastrofski, 1988; Mastrofski et al., 2007). It can be a mindset, but it can also be a set of very specific tactics and strategies. Here the term community-*oriented* is emphasized, as opposed to the term "community policing," because sometimes police can have the appearance of engaging the community but not be community oriented at all.

Skogan (2006) articulates three interrelated elements of community-oriented policing (COP): (1) citizen involvement in identifying and addressing public safety concerns, (2) the decentralization of decision making to develop responses to locally defined problems, and (3) problem solving. These activities go beyond programs that only inform communities about police activities or police programs that try and improve citizen satisfaction with the police (Trojanowicz et al., 1998). More recently, COP has encompassed notions of building collective efficacy and empowering community members (Sampson, 2011), as well as procedural justice and police legitimacy (Tyler, 1990). The goals of COP have included reducing fear, improving police-citizen relationships, increasing citizen involvement in public safety, reducing disorder, and increasing accountability and oversight of police by communities (Gill et al., 2014).

Many practices and programs have been associated with COP. These include officers and citizens collaborating to work on public safety problems in a neighborhood; community meetings in which police gain input from communities about both crime and policing problems; school-based programs in which officers try to connect with young people in various ways; neighborhood patrol programs where officers and citizens might patrol crime hot spots together; civilian oversight groups that may make recommendations about officer discipline or agency activities; or the application of community resources to address crime problems, to name a few. The ideals behind these activities are that citizens in democracies should have a say in how they are being policed and that police agents are accountable to the public in their actions and activities. Thus, for example, police would not be operating in a community-oriented manner if they did not share what they were doing about crime with members of the community (nor cared what the community thought), but rather set their own priorities about what problems to focus on (if at all) and how to focus on them. Such agencies would not be transparent or accountable to the community regarding their policies, practices, and spending, and also hide their internal affairs from the public.

In practice, even well-designed COP programs have several implementation challenges (see Mastrofski et al., 2007; Skogan, 2019). Both police officers and citizens may not know how to co-produce safety together (or even separately). Sustaining officer and citizen involvement in community-oriented programs can be challenging. In some communities, COP might be used by one group to oppress another, and marginalized groups may be left out of discussions altogether or even be the target of COP (Cheng, 2020). Even if citizens help to identify problems, problem-solving activities may be implemented poorly or lack resources to be implemented well.

Several reviews of the evaluation research on COP programs have been mixed in terms of COP's effectiveness. Two National Academies consensus committees have reviewed the research on COP (NASEM, 2018; NRC, 2004), arriving at similar conclusions as Gill and colleagues (2014) Campbell Systematic Review on COP. These reviews found that while community-oriented policing does not often have consistent crime-prevention or deterrence benefits, some programs can improve citizen satisfaction with police services (although the impacts on perceptions of police legitimacy may be weaker). However, we note that some COP activities, programs, and interventions have not been well defined or evaluated. For the evaluations that do exist, many are of modest methodological quality and do not measure long-term effects (NASEM, 2018).

One attempt to evaluate COP has been conducted by Evidence in Governance and Politics, a global research, evaluation, and learning network that fosters collaboration between academics and practitioners, with a focus on the Global South. The four year project was conducted in Brazil, Colombia, Liberia, Pakistan, the Philippines, and Uganda using common methodologies and building upon existing approaches in each country to implement a community-oriented policing program, using a problem-oriented policing model and engaging with the local community to share information.[3] Findings point to the need for an extended timeline for projects of this nature to ensure adequate time for relationship building on the ground with key stakeholders and for conclusive implementation, monitoring, and evaluation to be conducted. A steady presence of researchers and staff on the ground in the countries participating in the intervention was also an early indicator of promise in each country. Data from all countries, however, did not show changes in crime victimization, perceived future insecurity, citizen perceptions of police, police perceptions of citizens, police abuse, crime reporting, crime tips, or the reporting of police abuse. The architects of this study believe that community-oriented policing must be supported by large-scale structural reforms in order to yield greater success.

Whether COP can be implemented in sustainable ways that promote the rule of law and public safety remains to be seen. In places where public safety is needed most, community members may not have the time, resources, political power, or motivation to work with the police to coproduce public safety. Yet if they can work together on attaining protection of the public, a byproduct may be an increased legitimacy of policing, which in turn may support the rule of law—as the Northern Ireland case study suggests (see Box 4-2).

USE OF DISCRETION

A core aspect to the idea of public protection is the *reduction of harm*: how to minimize violence and subsequent harm in society, and how to minimize public harm when police use force to enforce the law. Many countries, and their policing traditions, place great value on public order and the prevention of ongoing conflicts, but they handle police discretion differently. In the United Kingdom, for example, the concept of discretion is at the heart of Common Law tradition since 1361. In response to the duty to keep the peace, police may use discretion *not* to exercise their state-granted authority to enforce the law, if that decision were likely to prevent harm. By the same token, a failure to enforce the law that then allows violence to erupt and cause harm would be a breach of peace-keeping duty.

The "pyramids of harm" model, with larger amounts of relatively harmless crimes at the base and smaller amounts of severe crimes at the peak, invites police leaders to concentrate officer time and activities where the smallest number of officers can prevent the greatest amount of victimization (Dudfield et al., 2017; Hiltz et al., 2020; Weinborn et al., 2017). This approach emphasizes the human rights principle of directing the greatest care to those in greatest need of protection. If 10 percent of victims are predicted to suffer 50 percent of the harm to be reported in the next 90

---

[3] See https://egap.org/our-work-0/the-metaketa-initiative/round4-community-policing.

> **BOX 4-2**
> **Police Reform in Northern Ireland (Workshop Presentation)**
>
> At the workshop, Stephen White, Human Rights Commission, emphasized the importance of community involvement and consultation, and community impact assessments. Such approaches to community policing are useful for a range of efforts: identifying root causes to a problem, assisting in change, operationalizing new tactics, gaining validity and legitimacy for policy development, or measuring success.
>
> Explaining Northern Ireland's checklist for police reform, White said that they put human rights and community service-oriented policing right in the center of their efforts from vision setting to recruitment to oversight and accountability. Every police officer at every rank had to go through mandatory human rights training, and is held to account by a code of ethics as well as criminal law.
>
> In terms of indicators for success in police reforms, White said that their macro target was increased community trust and more representation on the police force and accountability bodies of underrepresented groups of the community. He recognized that people and international bodies want to see indicators of success more quickly, but said the changes are more than just those visible in quantitative indicators. While there are more women and more Catholics in the police service today compared to previous decades, those indicators do not capture the full impact of reform efforts. Long-term investment is crucial in the interplay between increased trust and changing statistics. White noted that people may look at crime figures and other measurements hoping to see reductions in rates or other successes, but if there is more trust being built, sometimes crime figures will go up as people begin reporting more often. He cautioned that this context is important, and any research should reflect what is actually happening and any noteworthy impacts on relationships and accountability.
>
> White described the institutional design in which they gather and analyze community input in Northern Ireland. This open and transparent process of community engagement on public safety is called the community impact assessment. The most important piece is the decision log, which tracks those whom the police engaged with and the rationale for decisions. For example, if there are two different communities with competing demands in an area, police would need to ensure they engaged and consulted with members from both communities. This process would also need to document how comprehensive the consultation was, and how representative of the community those were with whom they consulted. A community, for this purpose, is a group of people within an area who have been adversely affected by an incident or are indirect victims of a particularly high-harm or shocking crime.
>
> ---
>
> NOTE: This speaker summary is presented as a factual accounting of what was presented at the workshop for the committee's consideration. The statements reflected here are those of the individual presenter and do not necessarily represent the views of all workshop participants or the committee.

days, police may legitimately be seen to have an option to invest 50 percent of resources in protecting those victims—despite its disruption of current activities that address far less harm. The discretion to allocate policing resources by predicted harm concentrations is the basis for using a "Crime Harm Index" to allocate police resources proactively for maximum crime prevention (Sherman et al., 2016). Note that this recommendation contrasts sharply with the idea of "broken windows" policing, where police resources devoted to minor offenses were hypothesized to lead to reductions in serious offenses.

The harm analysis needed to allocate resources in this way is widely available in the Global North, if not widely used. Yet, similar capacity to analyze risk and harm is present in Montevideo, Uruguay; Hyderabad, India; and Santiago, Chile (Sherman, 2021). The policy of triage in police resource allocation, applied both proactively and reactively, is one that may enhance public protection in many parts of the world already. With greater assistance in developing both data analysis and strategic planning, the strategy of prioritizing harm is one that could be tested around the globe.

CONCLUSION

Evidence-based proactive policing strategies, such as problem-oriented policing, community-oriented policing, and the use of discretion, which aim to reduce crime as well as the harm from severe crimes, seem particularly suited to promote the rule of law and public protection if carried out with an evidence-based approach. However, very few police agencies in any country have met the rigorous standards of an evidence-based approach outlined in Chapter 1.

Available research evidence has indicated that problem-oriented policing can be a promising strategy to reduce crime and disorder. Problem solving may be particularly effective at reducing crime when police target conditions, offenders, victims, and situations at specific locations and "hot spots" where crime concentrates. Recent reviews recognize that some community-oriented policing activities, programs, or interventions have not been well defined or evaluated. For the evaluations that do exist, many are of modest methodological quality and do not measure long-term effects. This research finds that while community-oriented policing does not often have consistent crime prevention or deterrence benefits, some programs can improve citizen satisfaction with police services. Whether any of the proactive policing strategies can demonstrate effects that promote the rule of law and public safety remains to be seen. See recommendations for a research agenda and infrastructure in the next chapter.

5

Conclusions and Recommendations

The challenges facing policing and police reform internationally are serious and significant. The quality of policing is a core test of the quality of good governance in ensuring the promotion of rule of law (ROL) and human rights to protect the public. Research on policing outcomes has grown in recent years (Neyroud, 2017, 2021). A great deal of this research comes from the Global North, and less from countries in the Global South. However, even in the Global North, police agencies have yet to develop ways of institutionalizing the application of such knowledge to their everyday policies and practices. Further, the great diversity of policing structures, policies, and practices across the countries with which the U.S. Department of State partners adds extra layers of complexity and challenge to international discussions of policing reform. All this raises more questions than answers about how existing knowledge can be transferred to contexts in the Global South.

Throughout this report, the committee has examined the state of the research on organizational policies, structures, and practices for policing. In doing so, it sought to consider whether certain policies, structures, and practices promote the ROL and protect the public better than others. It has shown the limits of applying existing evidence across a highly variable landscape of international policing.

Yet what this report has also shown is the success of research itself. Even as recently as a decade ago, there was no research available on several important police policies or practices. Now the body of research is growing from a wide variety of countries, with preliminary findings on a range of topics, including both descriptive analyses of police processes and functions and some evaluative work on the effects of various police practices, policies, and tactics on some sets of outcomes. What continues to be missing are evaluations of policing across different contexts and countries; standard measures of inputs, outputs, and effectiveness; a systematic account of underlying assumptions of such measures; and reliable counting of those measures.

This chapter outlines the committee's key findings from the existing body of evidence. It then presents a research agenda to expand knowledge and leverage an evidence-based approach to policing in order to institutionalize knowledge and build it into the basis of police practices in the years and decades to come.

TRANSLATING THE EVIDENCE: KEY IMPLICATIONS FOR PRACTICE

As noted in Chapter 1, to promote ROL and protect the population, an evidence-based policing approach requires: (1) a reliable body of knowledge about police practices; (2) the ongoing practice of evidence-based and systematic targeting, testing, and tracking in policing; and (3) the institutionalization and implementation of knowledge in police practices (Lum and Koper, 2017; Sherman, 2013). Incorporating and implementing practices grounded in research into police organizations requires translation, receptivity, and institutionalization. As noted in Chapter 1, even when research is translated, an evidence-based policing approach requires that foreign assistance donors and partner law enforcement agencies build receptivity to this knowledge, such that police officers and local leadership are amenable to it. Institutionalizing research and embedding it in practice then likely requires making fundamental adjustments to any police organization's systems and infrastructure of incentives, accountability, deployment, supervision, management, leadership, technology, and professional development to sustain an evidence-based approach over time.

In the endeavor to translate research into practice, the committee cautions that context is critical. Given the wide range of countries with whom INL works and to which findings from research might be applied, there can be a major challenge of contextual "fit." Programs that work in some countries may not work in others. The same tactics, strategies, and interventions that could be successfully used in one country may backfire in another (or even be used to oppress people or violate human rights). Even strong evidence that programs work in some countries may not be enough to predict what will work in others.

That perspective necessitates understanding and mapping out the barriers to change in each context. Planning the pathways to success before an innovation starts can also be aided by what Kahneman (2011) describes as a "pre-mortem" examination of a plan, asking "If this innovation dies in the attempt to implement it, what would be the most likely causes of death?" (pp. 264–265). Once barriers are identified, such knowledge may illuminate the choice for proceeding or not, or for proceeding with a plan for evading or overcoming those obstacles. The result would be a more selective targeting of different kinds of police reforms in different countries, based on feasibility as much as on need.

With these caveats in mind, the committee outlines the following key implications for donor practice, highlighting findings from the evidence detailed in previous chapters that can inform capacity-building efforts.

- Findings from available research regarding the role a militarized police plays in protecting the population are mixed and raise concerns about the consequences for the ROL. Militarization in the Mexican police has been associated with greater homicidal violence and human rights violations, but further study is needed to see if these findings hold outside the Mexican context. Studies in the United States have focused on crime reduction as an outcome, whether through transfer of military-grade weapons or SWAT-style teams, and their findings have been inconsistent. While one randomized controlled trial in Cali, Colombia, finds that crime decreased in the areas patrolled by the military, and researchers in Colombia and Mexico find that militarization appears to enjoy considerable public support, variations in local context may still lead the militarization of the police (or constabularization of the military) to cause more harm than it would prevent (see Chapter 2).
- The qualitative evidence on systems of police governance suggests that their effectiveness may strongly depend on whether they include dimensions of police operational independence and structures of checks and balances. There is no clear evidence about the effects of placing decision-making authority for police operations at higher or lower levels of government under national control, local control, or a combination of both. However, it is recognized that these choices may have inherent tradeoffs as it relates to policing practices (see Chapter 2).
- In places where the investigation of police misconduct is important for reform, a fair and anonymous system for submitting complaints is critical, since without a formal complaint a formal investigation is unlikely. Effective independent investigative agencies will likely foster public trust and increase government legitimacy by improving citizens' access to justice for crimes committed by state agents while ensuring due process for the accused (see Chapter 2).

- Accountability systems for tracking overall police performance and individual misconduct are critical to the ability of a police service to promote the ROL and thus protect the public from abuse by police. Thorough implementation of these systems, with checks and balances, seems very important. Studies also show that such efforts may require attention to cultural factors to be effective and avoid being thwarted directly by resistant parties or indirectly by cultural norms (see Chapter 3).
- Research has illuminated the promise of recruitment policies that promote a policing workforce representative of the community it serves and reflecting the diversity of its population. The consequences of such policies may improve police legitimacy and community confidence in the police by reducing hostility between police officers and citizens and elevating values of equal protection and respect both within and outside the police service. Recruitment policies can actively encourage the recruitment of underrepresented groups or remove structural obstacles to such recruitment. Retention policies are also needed, especially for retention of historically underrepresented identity groups, as such groups often have negative experiences within police agencies (see Chapter 3).
- Research suggests that several technologies may have the potential to increase police accountability to the ROL and their public safety mandates. However, achieving these outcomes depends on (1) whether police services have access to essential technologies that can fulfill such mandates, (2) how each technology is actually used (or not), (3) the strength and supervision of implementation policies concerning those technologies, and (4) whether citizens and the police share similar expectations about those technologies (see Chapter 3). For example, body-worn cameras may be an effective technology for accountability. However, this effectiveness relies on agencies having well-enforced policies that require police to turn on and use the cameras, as well as policies that dictate how the agency will process and actively use body-worn camera footage for internal and criminal investigations of suspect police actions (see Chapter 3).
- Internal police culture is likely to have significant consequences for external police engagement. Findings from recent correlational research are consistent: having policies aimed at creating a culture of accountability, fairness, and justice within a police department translates to positive effects on police interaction with the community (see Chapter 3).
- Research evidence shows that problem-oriented policing can be an effective practice to reduce crime and disorder, one component of

the ROL. Agencies often need critical infrastructure elements—such as information technologies and analytic resources—to implement and institutionalize a problem-solving approach in a consistent and meaningful way. However, even in low-resource communities, it would be possible to apply basic problem-solving skills and principles to collect and analyze available data and open communication channels to address chronic problems. An accountability infrastructure to record, document, and help assess problem-solving efforts would need to be developed and built into the police agency's rewards, incentives, and disciplinary subsystems. Problem-solving tactics and activities would also need to be monitored to ensure that they are not inadvertently harming the community, such as causing greater disparities or inequities in the justice system, or leading to greater police violence or uses of force (see Chapter 4).

- Several reviews of the evaluation research on community-oriented policing programs have been mixed in terms of their effectiveness at reducing crime. While community-oriented policing does not often have consistent crime prevention or deterrence benefits, some programs can improve citizen satisfaction with police services (although the impacts on perceptions of police legitimacy may be weaker, see Chapter 4).

These findings from the policing literature merit consideration for adoption in capacity-building programs to promote ROL and protection of the public. While there is much uncertainty on whether existing evidence can directly inform policing programs, existing evidence can be leveraged in capacity-building efforts to generate new knowledge if applied with intention and evaluated. There are also opportunities for assistance in amplifying lessons learned from research in international policing, including programs at the U.S. Departments of State, Justice, Treasury, and Homeland Security. To this end, "evidence partnerships" across various U.S. federal agencies, and between the United States and other countries undertaking similar activities, may be fruitful. In the committee's view, only the growth of INL's recent work in building new knowledge and reviewing existing lessons can provide sufficient clarity to fully answering the questions in our mandate and realizing the goal of translating evidence into practice.

A RESEARCH AGENDA FOR EVIDENCE-BASED POLICING

To facilitate greater adoption of evidence-based policing practices worldwide, a registry of global policing impact studies is also needed. While no such registry currently exists, such a registry could serve as a foundation for the development of both measurement methods and substantive conclusions that will advance qualitative and quantitative evidence and further inform practice.

> **RECOMMENDATION 1:** In pursuit of better knowledge management, foreign assistance donors, including the Bureau of International Narcotics and Law Enforcement Affairs, U.S. Department of State, should support the establishment of an open online registry of all available research worldwide on police organizational policies, structures, and practices with outcomes measuring the rule of law and public protection and analysis of contextual factors contributing to these outcomes.

The registry should be designed to manage documents in multiple languages and extend the knowledge accumulated to researchers across countries. Further, the registry should promote the growth of research in the countries within the Global South.

This registry could build on the work led by Mazerolle and colleagues (2017) for the University of Queensland's Global Policing Database, with a view to creating free public online access to the original research reports. Some features of the registry could support daily scanning of scientific journals and other sources for new research reports that can help to compile the "raw" knowledge from individual studies and scientific peer reviews of each study in order to provide a quality control check on all studies included. As part of the registry program, systematic reviews of all research registered in specific areas could be conducted periodically (e.g., a review of the effects of procedural justice training on police conduct with citizens). Effort will need to be made to group studies by country similarities (cultural or other relevant characteristics), as this can serve to aid moderator analyses in systematic reviews.

Existing training programs that discuss police organizational structures, policies, and practices need to reflect the available evidence related to organizational structures, policies, and practices and continue to adapt curricula as additional evidence emerges. Foreign assistance donors, such as the Bureau of International Narcotics and Law Enforcement Affairs, should examine their training in light of material and resources provided in this report and be prepared to continue to adapt curricula as new knowledge emerges.

> **RECOMMENDATION 2:** Foreign assistance donors, including the Bureau of International Narcotics and Law Enforcement Affairs, U.S. Department of State (INL), should conduct an evidence-based assessment of their training modules to determine how aligned the curricula are with available evidence on the outcomes of organizational structures,

policies, and practices that promote the rule of law and protection of the public and on the contexts in which such structures, policies, and practices work.

While the committee recognizes the wide range of curricula taught across the many countries with which INL works, given the knowledge already amassed in policing, INL needs to conduct an assessment of the curricula it funds in the Global South, including curricula taught in the International Law Enforcement Academies and other settings, to see if the content is aligned with current research knowledge. Part of that review would include an assessment of any curriculum's focus on evidence-based policing itself, to show how agencies might use existing evidence and learn how to institutionalize research into their everyday practices.

The committee recognizes that there are no simple answers to guide decisions around organizational policies, structures, and practices that promote rule of law and protect the population. Much organizational effectiveness depends on cultural, political, and social conditions, and such conditions can vary between and within countries. With better contextualization, many lessons from research in other countries can be tested for applicability in new settings. It would benefit donor efforts to have a better understanding of the conditions that affect the success of organizational-level interventions.

RECOMMENDATION 3: Foreign assistance donors should encourage, and possibly commission, research that examines the cultural, political, and social conditions in which police operate—and assesses which of the contextual variables are likely to lead to successful outcomes from different kinds of police assistance efforts.

As noted above, key gaps in the literature are evaluations of policing across different contexts and countries as well as standard measures of inputs, outputs, and effectiveness. These gaps are caused in part by the absence of a set of standards for the definition of effectiveness and reliable counting of those measures. Such standards are needed to interpret the meaning of research results (Sherman, 2012), as uncertainty over the reliability of measurement is a major impediment to translating science into practice. Foreign assistance donors are in a position to help facilitate the development of a research framework to assess policing interventions in multiple contexts as well as police-researcher partnerships to expand available policing research and advance evidence-based policing. Local research capacity exists in many countries, even in areas of high violence and civil unrest, but may lack the funding and incentives to form police-researcher partnerships. Donors can encourage police-research partnerships and facilitate police partnering with either extra-national research institutions or local researchers and provide the necessary technical assistance to conduct research and evaluations of interventions.

> RECOMMENDATION 4: To gather data and expand available policing research, foreign assistance donors, including the Bureau of International Narcotics and Law Enforcement Affairs, U.S. Department of State, should incentivize partner countries to monitor, track, and evaluate the implementation of promising approaches and other initiatives by linking resources to establish police-research partnerships in assistance agreements.

The challenge of deciding how much aid each country receives is based on a variety of factors, many of which are political in nature and thus outside the scope of our task. However, to advance the long-term, overall strategy of global police reform, it is essential to create a vanguard of cooperating countries that implement evidence-based policing more comprehensively and substantially than most police agencies in the Global North have done to date. Investing in local partners who are willing to do the evidence and data gathering work is essential. The State Department is uniquely positioned to incentivize and facilitate such reform.

A reliable infrastructure for evidence-based policing is one based on international standards and metrics. This report has repeatedly noted the need for reliable records management for all kinds of police operations, and not just for reported deaths. It has also noted major gaps in that reliability in the Global North as well as the Global South.

> RECOMMENDATION 5: To advance a policing research framework suitable for multiple countries, foreign assistance donors should raise awareness in host countries of the value of recording and reporting crime and harm metrics. In addition, they should encourage the research community to establish a model crime reporting system for violent crimes and the identification of geographic concentrations of harm from crime and disorder to strengthen understanding of both crime and how officers are responding to crime across countries.

The goal of a model crime reporting system would be to identify specific pieces of information that must be collected so that police agencies can more successfully carry out the protection of the public. Such a system could be based on the World Health Organization's Violence Prevention

Alliance,[1] which includes standards for recording crime reports, for independent (nonpolice) auditing of compliance with those standards, and for regular reports to the public on the results of those audits. This system would need to be translated into the language(s) of each state the U.S. government is assisting and installed in a software package that can be operated as locally, regionally, or nationally as different countries may require.

Similarly, a model recording and reporting system for identifying patterns and concentrations of harm may use a globally constant crime severity or harm index. This system, in order to support both preventive operations and reliable research, could include unique identifiers for places, victims, suspects, and systematic evidence of social network links in crime records across individuals. The aim of such crime analysis would be to understand where, when, and who commits crimes as a way to better understand safety concerns, with the ultimate purpose of better targeting of effective practices. These records could be used to support a wide range of initiatives in evidence-based policing, problem-oriented policing, and community-oriented policing. At the same time, because concentrating crime prevention efforts on specific places or people may disproportionately concentrate police attention on certain populations, such efforts must be combined with a comparable concentration of officer training, incentivizing, and monitoring to protect against human rights violations.

In order to create the capacity for reliable assessments of change over time and differences across countries in the level of crime harm, this system could adopt a system already used in Canada, New Zealand, the United Kingdom, and parts of Australia that provides a standard weight for each of the major crime types. Despite differences in sentencing practices across countries, it is not unreasonable to select a standard weighting system for analytic purposes only (and not to promote a standard sentencing system). This standard would be applied only to the most serious offenses, such as murder, rape, grievous bodily harm, robbery, and aggravated assault. One option is to use the midpoint between average sentences and sentencing guidelines (which leave out prior offender records as a sentencing criterion). These two official sources reflect different methodological perspectives, both of which can be combined by selecting a midpoint; the use of guidelines is known as the Cambridge Crime Harm Index (Sherman, Neyroud, and Neyroud, 2016). Alternatively, agencies could use monetary-based harm estimates based on meta-analyses of public surveys, jury awards, and variation in home values, such as the RAND Cost of Crime Calculator (Heaton, 2010). Once harm weightings are applied across countries, the comparisons of public protection will become more reliable, even while

---

[1] See https://www.who.int/violenceprevention/approach/definition/en.

remaining far from perfect. It would be a first step in a long journey to global transparency about crime and justice.

The creation of transparent facts about crime and policing can be highly disruptive in any political context. Establishing equal protection by improving police recording practices is a major issue for the rule of law. It is also a major operational and diplomatic challenge, as suppression of crime reports is an inconvenient truth. Understanding the successes and failures of reporting systems will comprise a major step forward in the global understanding of how to achieve a safer and more lawful world.

References

Amaral, S., Bhalotra, S., and Prakash, N. (2021). *Gender, Crime and Punishment: Evidence from Women Police Stations in India*. The Institute for Economic Development Working Papers Series dp-309. Boston, MA: Boston University, Department of Economics.

Andersen, H.A., and Mueller-Johnson, K. (2018). The Danish crime harm index: How it works and why it matters. *Cambridge Journal of Evidence-Based Policing, 2*(1-2), 52–69.

Andersson, C., and Kazemian, L. (2018). Reliability and validity of cross-national homicide data: A comparison of UN and WHO data. *International Journal of Comparative and Applied Criminal Justice, 42*(4), 287–302.

Ariel, B., Farrar, W.A., and Sutherland, A. (2015). The effect of police body-worn cameras on use of force and citizens' complaints against the police: A randomized controlled trial. *Journal of Quantitative Criminology, 31*(3), 509–535.

Arriola, L.R., Dow, D.A., Matanock, A.M., and Mattes, M. (2021). Policing institutions and post-conflict peace. *Journal of Conflict Resolution*, May. https://doi.org/10.1177/00220027211013088.

Barnes, G.C., Williams, S., Sherman, L.W., Parmar, J., House, P., and Brown, S.A. (2020). *Sweet Spots of Residual Deterrence: A Randomized Crossover Experiment in Minimalist Police Patrol*. Soc ARCiV. https://osf.io/preprints/socarxiv/kwf98.

Basford, L., Sims, C., Agar, I., and Harinam, V. (2021). Effects of one-a-day foot patrols on hot spots of serious violence and crime harm: A randomized crossover trial. *Cambridge Journal of Evidence-Based Policing, 5*(4).

Bayley, D.H. (1985). *Patterns of Policing: A Comparative International Analysis*. New Brunswick, NJ: Rutgers University Press.

Bayley, D.H. (2006). *Changing the Guard: Developing Democratic Police Abroad*. Oxford University Press.

Bergmann, A., Ojeda, A.R., Forné, C.S., Correa, C.P., Marques, D., Velasquez, H.A., Cano, I., Muñoz, J.C., Ávila, K., Rueda, M.S., Nunes, S.B., and Husek, T. (2019). *Monitor of Use of Lethal Force in Latin America: A Comparative Study of Brazil, Colombia, El Salvador, Mexico, and Venezuela*. Open Society Foundations. https://www.monitorfuerzaletal.com/Executive-Monitor-English.pdf.

Bingham, T. (2011). *The Rule of Law*. Penguin UK.
Bittner, E. (1974). A theory of police: Florence nightingale in pursuit of Willie Sutton. In *The Potential for Reform of Criminal Justice*, (Ed.). Beverly Hills, CA: Sage.
Black, D.J. (1970). Production of crime rates. *American Sociological Review*, 733–748.
Blair, R., and Morse, B. (2021). Policing and the legacies of wartime state predation: Evidence from a survey and field experiment in Liberia. *Journal of Conflict Resolution*.
Blair, R., and Weintraub, M. (2020). *Mano Dura: An Experimental Evaluation of the Plan Fortaleza Program in Cali, Colombia*. https://osf.io/95cz3.
Blair, R., and Weintraub, M. (2021). Military policing exacerbates crime and human rights abuses: A randomized controlled trial in Cali, Colombia. http://dx.doi.org/10.2139/ssrn.3925245.
Bland, M.P., Leggetter, M., Cestaro, R., and Sebire, J. (2021). Fifteen minutes per day keeps the violence away: A crossover randomized controlled trial on the impact of foot patrols on serious violence in large hot spot areas. *Cambridge Journal of Evidence-Based Policing*, 5(3).
Bordua, D., and Reiss, A. (1966). Command, control, and charisma: Reflections on police bureaucracy. *American Journal of Sociology*, 72(1), 68–76.
Borges, M., Gans-Morse, J., Makarin, A., Nickow, A., Prasad, M., Watters, V., Mannah-Blankson, T., and Zhang, D. (2017). *Combatting Corruption Among Civil Servants: Interdisciplinary Perspectives on What Works*. USAID Research and Innovations Grants Working Paper Series. Washington, DC: U.S. Agency for International Development.
Bottoms, A.E., and Tankebe, J. (2017). *Police Legitimacy and the Authority of the State*. Hart Publishing Limited.
Bove, V., and Gavrilova, E. (2017). Police officer on the frontline or a soldier? The effect of police militarization on crime. *American Economic Journal: Economic Policy*, 9(3), 1–18.
Bradford, B., and Quinton, P. (2014). Self-legitimacy, police culture and support for democratic policing in an English constabulary. *British Journal of Criminology*, 54(6), 1023–1046.
Bradford, B., Quinton, P., Myhill, A., and Porter, G. (2014). Why do 'the law' comply? Procedural justice, group identification and officer motivation in police organizations. *European Journal of Criminology*, 11(5), 110–131.
Braga, A.A., and Bond, B.J. (2008). Policing crime and disorder hot spots: A randomized controlled trial. *Criminology*, 46(3), 577–608.
Braga, A.A., and Weisburd, D.L. (2006). Problem-oriented policing: The disconnect between principles and practice. *Police Innovation: Contrasting Perspectives*, 133–154. New York: Cambridge University Press.
Braga, A.A., and Weisburd, D.L. (2012). The effects of focused deterrence strategies on crime: A systematic review and meta-analysis of the empirical evidence. *Journal of Research in Crime & Delinquency*, 49(3), 323–358.
Braga, A.A., Turchan, B., Papachristos, A.V., and Hureau, D.M. (2019). Hot spots policing of small geographic areas effects on crime. *Campbell Systematic Reviews*, 15(3), e1046.
Brantingham, P.L., and Brantingham, P.J. (1993). Environment, routine and situation: Toward a pattern theory of crime. *Advances in Criminological Theory*, 5, 259–294.
Broidy, M., and Prenzler, T. (2020). The New Zealand police early intervention system: A review of implementation and impact issues. *International Journal of Police Science & Management*, 22(3), 297–307. https://doi.org/10.1177/1461355720931891.
Brooks, L. (2008). Volunteering to be taxed: Business improvement districts and the extra-governmental provision of public safety. *Journal of Public Economics*, 92(1-2), 388–406.
Carrington, K., Guala, N., Puyol, M.V., and Sozzo, M. (2020). How women's police stations empower women, widen access to justice and prevent gender violence. *International Journal for Crime, Justice and Social Democracy*, 9(1), 42–67.

REFERENCES

Chalmers, I. (2003). Trying to do more good than harm in policy and practice: The role of rigorous, transparent, up-to-date evaluations. *The ANNALS of the American Academy of Political and Social Science, 589*(1), 22–40.

Chan, J., Brereton, D., Legosz, M., and Doran, S. (2001). *E-policing: The Impact of Information Technology on Police Practices.* Brisbane, Australia: Queensland Criminal Justice Commission.

Cheng, C., and Long, W. (2018). Improving police services: Evidence from the French quarter task force. *Journal of Public Economics, 164*, 1–18.

Cheng, T. (2020). Input without influence: The silence and scripts of police and community relations. *Social Problems, 67*(1), 171–189.

Cheung, A.Y. (2019). *Measuring the Measures: Rule of Law Indices and Abusive Legalism.* https://doi.org/10.31228/osf.io/8r5zb.

Clarke, R.V. (Eds.). (1997). *Situational Crime Prevention: Successful Case Studies* (2nd ed.). Albany, NY: Harrow & Heston.

Clarke, R.V.G., and Felson, M. (1993). *Routine Activity and Rational Choice 5.* Transaction Publishers.

Cook, P.J., and MacDonald, J. (2011). Public safety through private action: An economic assessment of bids. *The Economic Journal, 121*(552), 445–462.

Dammert, L., and Bailey, J. (2005). Reforma policial y participación military en el combate a la delincuencia. *Fuerzax Armadas y Sociedad, 19*(1), 133–152.

Dell, M. (2015). Trafficking networks and the Mexican drug war. *American Economic Review, 105*(6), 1738–1779.

Dudfield, G., Angel, C., Sherman, L.W., and Torrence, S. (2017). The "power curve" of victim harm: Targeting the distribution of crime harm index values across all victims and repeat victims over 1 year. *Cambridge Journal of Evidence-Based Policing, 1*(1), 38–58.

Eck, J.E. and Rosenbaum, D.P. (1994). The new police order: Effectiveness, equity, and efficiency in community policing. *The Challenge of Community Policing: Testing the Promises,* 3–26. Thousand Oaks, CA: Sage.

Eck, J.E., and Spelman, W. (1987). *Problem-Solving: Problem-Oriented Policing in Newport News.* Washington, DC: Police Executive Research Forum.

Eck, J.E., and Wartell, J. (1998). Improving the management of rental properties with drug problems: A randomized experiment. *Crime Prevention Studies, 9*, 161–185.

Eck, J.E., and Weisburd, D.L. (1995). Crime places in crime theory. *Crime and Place: Crime Prevention Studies,* 1–34. Monsey, NY: Criminal Justice Press and the Police Executive Research Forum.

Engel, R.S., and Worden, R.E. (2003). Police officers' attitudes, behavior, and supervisory influences: An analysis of problem solving. *Criminology, 41*(1), 131–166.

Espinosa, V., and Rubin, D.B. (2015). Did the military interventions in the Mexican drug war increase violence? *The American Statistician, 69.*

Fariss, C., Kenwick, M., and Reuning, K. (2020). Latent Human Rights Protection Scores Version 4. *Harvard Dataverse.* https://doi.org/10.7910/DVN/RQ85GK.

Faull, A. (2010). 'When I see them I feel like beating them': Corruption and the South African police service. *South African Crime Quarterly, 34*, 33–40.

Flores-Macías, G. (2018). The consequences of militarizing anti-drug efforts for state capacity in Latin America: Evidence from Mexico. *Comparative Politics, 51*(1), 1–20.

Flores-Macías, G.A., and Zarkin, J. (2019). The militarization of law enforcement: Evidence from Latin America. *Perspectives on Politics,* 1–20.

———. (2020). *The Consequences of Militarization for Human Rights: Evidence from Mexico.* Working Paper, Cornell University.

———. (2021). Militarization and perceptions of law enforcement in the developing world: Evidence from a conjoint experiment in Mexico. *British Journal of Political Science*, 52(3), 1377–1397. https://doi.org/10.1017/S0007123421000259.

Gerber, T.P., and Mendelson, S.E. (2008). Public experiences of police violence and corruption in contemporary Russia: A case of predatory policing? *Law & Society Review*, 42(1), 1–44.

Gill, C., Weisburd, D.L., Telep, C.W., Vitter, Z., and Bennett, B. (2014). Community-oriented policing to reduce crime, disorder and fear and increase satisfaction and legitimacy among citizens: A systematic review. *Journal of Experimental Criminology*, 10(4), 399–428.

Gladwell, M. (2019). *Talking to Strangers: What We Should Know About the People We Don't Know*. Penguin UK.

Goldstein, H. (1979). Improving policing: A problem-oriented approach. *Crime & Delinquency*, 25(2), 236–258.

———. (1990). *Problem-Oriented Policing*. New York: McGraw-Hill.

González, Y.M. (2020). *Authoritarian Police in Democracy: Contested Security in Latin America*. New York: Cambridge University Press.

Greene, J.R. (2000). *Community Policing in America: Changing the Nature, Structure, and Function of the Police*, 3. https://www.ncjrs.gov/criminal_justice2000/vol_3/03g.pdf.

Greene, J.R., and Mastrofski, S. (Eds.). (1988). *Community Policing: Rhetoric or Reality*. New York: Praeger.

Gunderson, A., Cohen, E., Schiff, K.J., Clark, T.S., Glynn, A.N., and Owens, M.L. (2021). Counterevidence of crime-reduction effects from federal grants of military equipment to local police. *Nature Human Behaviour, 5*.

Hagan, J., and Haugh, T. (2011). Ethnic cleaning as euphemism, metaphor, criminology, and law. In L.N. Sadat (Eds.), *Forging a Convention for Crime against Humanity and Law*, 202–222. New York: Cambridge University Press.

Harris, C.J., and Worden, R.E. (2014). The effect of sanctions on police misconduct. *Crime & Delinquency*, 60(8), 1258–1288.

Harris, M.C., Park, J., Bruce, D.J., and Murray, M.N. (2017). Peacekeeping force: Effects of providing tactical equipment to local law enforcement. *American Economic Journal: Economic Policy*, 9(3), 291–313.

Heaton, P. (2010). *Hidden in Plain Sight: What Cost-of-Crime Research Can Tell Us About Investing in Police*. Washington, DC: RAND Corporation.

Herbert, S. (2006). Tangled up in blue: Conflicting paths to police legitimacy. *Theoretical Criminology*, 10(4), 481–504.

Hills, A. (2012). Lost in translation: Why Nigeria's police don't implement democratic reforms. *International Affairs*, 88(4), 739–755.

Hills, A. (2020). The dynamics of prototypical police forces: Lessons from two Somali cities. *International Affairs*, 96(6), 1527–1546.

Hiltz, N., Bland, M., and Barnes, G.C. (2020). Victim-offender overlap in violent crime: Targeting crime harm in a Canadian suburb. *Cambridge Journal of Evidence-Based Policing*, 4(3), 114–124.

Hinkle, J.C., Weisburd, D., Telep, C.W., and Petersen, K. (2020). Problem-oriented policing for reducing crime and disorder: An updated systematic review and meta-analysis. *Campbell Systematic Reviews*, 16(2), e1089. https://doi.org/10.1002/cl2.1089.

House, P.D., and Neyroud, P.W. (2018). Developing a crime harm index for Western Australia: The WACHI. *Cambridge Journal of Evidence-Based Policing*, 2(1), 70–94.

REFERENCES

Jones, G.J. (2018). *Enhancing Patrol Management Strategy and Deployment Efficiency of Police Managers by Utilizing Automated Vehicle Locator (AVL) Technology.* Ph.D. Dissertation. Fairfax, VA: George Mason University.

Kahneman, D. (2011). *Thinking, Fast and Slow.* NY: Macmillan.

Karim, S. (2019). Restoring confidence in post-conflict security sectors: Survey evidence from Liberia on female ratio balancing reforms. *British Journal of Political Science, 49*(3), 799–821.

Karim, S., Gilligan, M.J., Blair, R., and Beardsley, K. (2018). International gender balancing reforms in postconflict countries: Lab-in-the-field evidence from the Liberian national police. *International Studies Quarterly, 62*(3), 618–631.

Kärrholm, F., Neyroud, P. and Smaaland, J. (2020). Designing the Swedish crime harm index: An evidence-based strategy. *Cambridge Journal of Evidence-Based Policing,* 1–19.

Koper, C.S. (1995). Just enough police presence: Reducing crime and disorderly behavior by optimizing patrol time in crime hot spots. *Justice Quarterly, 12*(4), 649–672.

Koper, C.S., Lum, C., and Willis, J.J. (2014). Optimizing the use of technology in policing: Results and implications from a multi-site study of the social, organizational, and behavioural aspects of implementing police technologies. *Policing: A Journal of Policy and Practice, 8*(2), 212–221.

Koper, C.S., Lum, C., Willis, J.J., Woods, D.J., and Hibdon, J. (2015). *Realizing the Potential of Technology in Policing: A Multi-Site Study of the Social, Organizational, and Behavioral Aspects of Implementing Policing Technologies.* Washington, DC: U.S. Department of Justice, National Institute of Justice. https://www.ojp.gov/ncjrs/virtual-library/abstracts/realizing-potential-technology-policing-multisite-study-social.

Lewin K. (1951). *Field Theory in Social Science.* London: Harper Row.

Lowande, K. (2021). Police demilitarization and violent crime. *Nature Human Behaviour, 5.*

Lum, C. (2009). *Translating Police Research into Practice.* Washington, DC: U.S. Department of Justice, Office of Justice Programs. https://www.ojp.gov/ncjrs/virtual-library/abstracts/evidence-based-policing-translating-research-practice.

Lum, C., and Koper, C.S. (2017). *Evidence-Based Policing: Translating Research into Practice.* New York: Oxford University Press.

Lum, C., Koper, C.S., and Willis, J. (2017). Understanding the limits of technology's impact on police effectiveness. *Police Quarterly, 20*(2), 135–163.

Lum, C., Koper, C.S., Wilson, D.B., Stoltz, M., Goodier, M., Eggins, E., Higginson, A., and Mazerolle, L. (2020). Body-worn cameras' effects on police officers and citizen behavior: A systematic review. *Campbell Systematic Reviews* 16(3), e1112.

Macbeth, E., and Ariel, B. (2019). Place-based statistical versus clinical predictions of crime hot spots and harm locations in Northern Ireland. *Justice Quarterly, 36*(1), 93–126.

Macintyre, S., Prenzler, T., and Chapman, J. (2008). Early intervention to reduce complaints: An Australian Victoria Police Initiative. *Policing: An International Journal of Police Science and Management, 10*(2), 238–250.

Masera, F. (2019). Police safety, killings by the police and the militarization of us law enforcement. *SSRN Electronic Journal.* http://dx.doi.org/10.2139/ssrn.3342922.

Masera, F. (2021). Violent crime and the overmilitarization of U.S. policing. *The Journal of Law, Economics, and Organization.* https://doi.org/10.1093/jleo/ewaa021.

Mastrofski, S.D., Willis, J.J., and Kochel, T.R. (2007). The challenges of implementing community policing in the United States. *Policing: A Journal of Policy and Practice, 1*(2), 223–234.

Mazerolle, L., Eggins, E., Higginson, A., and Stanko, B. (2017). Evidence-based policing as a disruptive innovation: The Global Policing Database as a disruption tool. *Advances in Evidence-Based Policing,* Crime Science Series, 117–138. London: Routledge.

Mazerolle, L., Price, J., and Roehl, J. (2000). Civil remedies and drug control: A randomized field trial in Oakland, CA. *Evaluation Review,* 24(2), 212–241.

McCoy, T. (2021). Rio police were ordered to limit favela raids during the pandemic. They're still killing hundreds of people. *The Washington Post.* https://www.washingtonpost.com/world/2021/05/20/brazil-police-rio-jacarezinho-favela-raid/.

Miller, A.R., and Segal, C. (2018). Do female officers improve law enforcement quality?: Effects on crime reporting and domestic violence. *The Review of Economics Studies,* 86(5), 2220–2247.

Miller, W.R. (1977). *Cops and Bobbies: Police Authority in New York and London, 1830–1870.* Chicago: University of Chicago Press.

Moncada, E. (2016). *Cities, Business, and the Politics of Urban Violence in Latin America.* Stanford University Press.

Muggah, R., Garzón, J.C., and Suárez, M. (2018). *Mano Dura: 2018. The Costs and Benefits of Repressive Criminal Justice for Young People in Latin America.* Igarapé Institute.

Mummolo, J. (2018). Militarization fails to enhance police safety or reduce crime but may harm police reputation. *Proceedings of the National Academy of Sciences,* 115(37).

National Academies of Sciences, Engineering, and Medicine (NASEM). (2018). *Proactive Policing: Effects on Crime and Communities.* Washington, DC: The National Academies Press.

National Research Council. (1993). *Understanding and Preventing Violence: Volume 1.* Washington, DC: National Academy Press.

_____. (2004). *Fairness and Effectiveness in Policing: The Evidence.* Washington, DC: The National Academies Press.

_____. (2005). *Firearms and Violence: A Critical Review.* Washington, DC: The National Academies Press.

Neyroud, P.W. (2017). *Learning to Field Test in Policing: Using an Analysis of Completed Randomised Controlled Trials Involving the Police to Develop a Grounded Theory on the Factors Contributing to High Levels of Treatment Integrity in Police Field Experiments.* Doctoral dissertation, University of Cambridge.

Neyroud, P. (2021). *Policing "Landscapes" for the Rule of Law and Public Protection: A Review of the Available Evidence on Organizational Policies, Structures, and Human Resources.* Paper prepared for the Committee on the Evidence to Advance Reform in the Global Security and Justice Sectors, National Academies of Sciences, Engineering, and Medicine. https://www.nationalacademies.org/event/03-24-2021/evidence-to-advance-reform-in-the-global-security-and-justice-sectors-workshop-1-public-session-1.

O'Connor, D. (2021). *Translation of the Rule of Law.* Presentation to the Committee on the Evidence to Advance Reform in the Global Security and Justice Sectors, National Academies of Sciences, Engineering, and Medicine. https://www.nationalacademies.org/event/03-25-2021/evidence-to-advance-reform-in-the-global-security-and-justice-sectors-workshop-1-public-session-2.

O'Donnell, G. (2004). The quality of democracy: Why the rule of law matters. *Journal of Democracy,* 15(4), 32–46.

Oliver, W.M. (2017). *August Vollmer: The Father of American Policing.* Carolina Academic Press.

Olken, B.A. (2007). Monitoring corruption: Evidence from a field experiment in Indonesia. *Journal of Political Economy,* 115(2), 200–249.

Orlikowski, W.J., and Gash, D.C. (1994). Technological frames: Making sense of information technology in organizations. *ACM Transactions on Information Systems (TOIS),* 12(2), 174–207.

Owens, E., and Ba, B.A. (2021). The economics of policing and public safety. *The Journal of Economic Perspectives,* 35(4), 3-28.

Perova, E., and Reynolds, S.A. (2017). Women's police stations and intimate partner violence: Evidence from Brazil. *Social Science & Medicine, 174*, 188–196.

Pion-Berlin, D., and Carreras, M. (2017). Armed forces, police and crime-fighting in Latin America. *Journal of Politics in Latin America, 9*(3), 3–26.

Prenzler, T., and Sinclair, G. (2013). The status of women police officers: An international review. *International Journal of Law, Crime and Justice 41*(2), 115–131.

Rajah, V.K. (2012). Panel discussion: Measuring the rule of law. *Singapore Journal of Legal Studies*, 331–356. http://www.jstor.org/stable/24872215.

Reiss, A.J., Jr. (1971). *The Police and the Public.* New Haven, CT: Yale University Press.

Robey, D., Boudreau, M.C., and Rose, G.M. (2000). Information technology and organizational learning: A review and assessment of research. *Accounting, Management and Information Technologies, 10*(2), 125–155.

Rothwell, S. (2021). *Immediate Phone Service vs. Intended Police Visits: Caller Satisfaction and Cost-Effectiveness in a Randomised Trial.* [Unpublished masters thesis]. Institute of Criminology, University of Cambridge.

Sampson, R.J. (2011). The community. *Crime and Public Policy* (2nd ed.), 210–236. New York: Oxford University Press.

Sanders, C., and Condon, C. (2017). Crime analysis and cognitive effects: The practice of policing through flows of data. *Global Crime, 18*(3), 237–255.

Sanders, C., and Sheptycki, J. (2017). Policing, crime and 'big data'; towards a critique of the moral economy of stochastic governance. *Crime, Law and Social Change, 68*(1), 1–15.

Scheffer, D. (2011). Crimes against humanity and the responsibility to protect. *Forging a Convention for Crime against Humanity and Law*, 305–322. New York: Cambridge University Press.

Sherman, L.W. (1978). *Scandal and Reform: Controlling Police Corruption.* University of California Press.

———. (1990). Police crackdowns: Initial and residual deterrence. *Crime and Justice, 12*, 1–48.

———. (1998). *Evidence-Based Policing.* Ideas in American Policing Series. Washington, DC: Police Foundation. https://www.policefoundation.org/wp-content/uploads/2015/06/Sherman-1998-Evidence-Based-Policing.pdf.

———. (2011). *Professional Policing and Liberal Democracy: The 2011 Benjamin Franklin Medal Lecture.* London: The Royal Society for the Encouragement of Arts, Manufactures and Commerce. https://www.crim.cam.ac.uk/system/files/documents/franklinfinal2011.pdf.

———. (2012). *Developing and Evaluating Citizen Security Programs in Latin America: A Protocol for Evidence-Based Crime Prevention.* Washington, DC: IADB.

———. (2013). The rise of evidence-based policing: Targeting, testing, and tracking. *Crime and Justice, 42*(1), 377–451.

———. (2015). *Reducing Deadly Force in U.S. Policing: A View from England and Wales.* Statement to the Presidential Task Force on 21st Century Policing, Washington, DC. https://www.cambridge-ebp.co.uk/research-1.

———. (2021). The Cambridge Police Executive Programme: A global reach for pracademics. In E. Piza and B. Welsh (Eds.), *The Globalization of Evidence-Based Policing: Innovations in Bridging the Research-Practice Divide.* London: Routledge.

Sherman, L.W., Buerger, M., and Gartin, P. (1989). *Beyond Dial-A-Cop: A Randomized Test of Repeat Call Address Policing (RECAP).* Washington, DC: Crime Control Institute. https://static1.squarespace.com/static/5d809efd96f5c906aaf61f3d/t/5f9270e7497b39456c8272d2/1603432683699/Sherman+RECAP+report+89.pdf.

Sherman, L.W., Gartin, P., and Buerger, M. (1989). Hot spots of predatory crime: Routine activities and the criminology of place. *Criminology, 27*(1), 27–56.

Sherman, L., Neyroud, P.W., and Neyroud, E. (2016). The Cambridge crime harm index: Measuring total harm from crime based on sentencing guidelines. *Policing: A Journal of Policy and Practice, 10*(3), 171–183.

Shjarback, J.A. (2015). Emerging early intervention systems: An agency-specific pre-post comparison of formal citizen complaints of use of force. *Policing: A Journal of Policy and Practice, 9*(4), 314–325.

Shjarback, J.A. (2021). Early intervention systems. In R.G. Dunham, G.P. Alpert, and K.D. McLean (Eds.), *Critical Issues in Policing: Contemporary Readings* (8th ed.), 655–667. Long Grove, IL: Waveland Press, Inc.

Skogan, W.G. (2006). Asymmetry in the impact of encounters with police. *Policing and Society, 16*(2), 99–126.

_____. (2019). Community policing. In D. Weisburd and A. Braga (Eds.), *Police Innovation: Contrasting Perspectives*, (2nd ed.). New York: Cambridge University Press.

Soares, R.R., and Viveiros, I. (2017). Organization and information in the fight against crime: An evaluation of the integration of police forces in the state of Minas Gerais, Brazil. *Journal of the Latin American and Caribbean Economic Association, 17*(2), 29–63.

Sutherland, J., and Mueller-Johnson, K. (2019). Evidence vs. professional judgment in ranking "power few" crime targets: A comparative analysis. *Cambridge Journal of Evidence-Based Policing, 3*(1), 54–72.

Tankebe, J. (2010). Identifying the correlates of police organizational commitment in Ghana. *Police Quarterly, 13*(1), 73–91.

Taylor, B., Koper, C., and Woods, D. (2011). A randomized controlled trial of different policing strategies at hot spots of violent crime. *Journal of Experimental Criminology, 7*(2), 149–181.

Terrill, W., and Ingram, J.R. (2016). Citizen complaints against the police: An eight city examination. *Police Quarterly, 19*(2), 150–179.

Trinkner, R., Tyler, T.R., and Goff, P.A. (2016). Justice from within: The relations between a procedurally just organizational climate and police organizational efficiency, endorsement of democratic policing, and officer well-being. *Psychology, Public Policy, and Law, 22*(2), 158–172.

Trojanowicz, R.C., Kappeler, V.E., Gaines, L.K., Bucqueroux, B., and Sluder, R. (1998). *Community Policing: A Contemporary Perspective*, (2nd ed.) Cincinnati, OH: Anderson Publishing.

Tyler, T.R. (1990). *Why People Obey the Law*. New Haven, CT: Yale University Press.

U.S. Department of State. (2016). *INL Guide to Police Assistance*. Washington, DC: U.S. Department of State, Bureau of International Narcotics and Law Enforcement Affairs. https://2009-2017.state.gov/documents/organization/263419.pdf.

Versteeg, M., and Ginsburg, T. (2017). Measuring the rule of law: A comparison of indicators. *Law & Social Inquiry, 42*(1), 100–137. https://doi.org/10.1111/lsi.12175.

Walker, S. (2001). *Police Accountability: The Role of Citizen Oversight*. Belmont, CA: Wadsworth.

Walker, S. (2005). *The New World of Police Accountability*. Thousand Oaks, CA: Sage.

Walker, S., and Milligan, S. (2005). *Supervision and Intervention Within Early Intervention Systems: A Guide for Law Enforcement Chief Executives*. Washington, DC: Police Executive Research Forum.

Walker, S., Alpert, G.P., and Kenney, D. (2001). *Early Warning Systems: Responding to the Problem Police Officer*. Washington, DC: U.S. Department of Justice, National Institute of Justice.

Weinborn, C., Ariel, B., Sherman, L.W., and O'Dwyer, E. (2017). Hotspots vs. harmspots: Shifting the focus from counts to harm in the criminology of place. *Applied Geography, 86*, 226–244.

Weisburd, D.L., Telep, C.W., Hinkle, J.C., and Eck, J.E. (2010). Is problem-oriented policing effective in reducing crime and disorder? Findings from a Campbell systematic review. *Criminology & Public Policy*, 9(1), 139–172.

White, S. (2021). *Police Organizational Policies to Promote the Rule of Law and Protect the Population—in the International Context.* Presentation to the Committee on the Evidence to Advance Reform in the Global Security and Justice Sectors, National Academies of Sciences, Engineering, and Medicine, March 24, 2021. https://www.nationalacademies.org/event/03-24-2021/evidence-to-advance-reform-in-the-global-security-and-justice-sectors-workshop-1-public-session-1.

Worden, R.E., Kim, M., Harris, C.J., Pratte, M.A., Dorn, S.E. and Hyland, S.S. (2013). Intervention with problem officers: An outcome evaluation of an EIS intervention. *Criminal Justice and Behavior*, 40(4), 409–437.

Zempi, I. (2020). 'Looking back, I wouldn't join up again': The lived experiences of police officers as victims of bias and prejudice perpetrated by fellow staff within an English police force. *Police Practice and Research*, 21(1), 33–48.

Appendix A

Validation Exercise

This appendix discusses and compares two of the most comprehensive indices of the rule of law (ROL): (a) the World Justice Project (WJP)[1] and (b) the Varieties of Democracies (V-DEM) Project.[2] Both projects provide a composite ROL Index through a multidimensional set of outcome indicators, each of which reflects a particular aspect of this complex concept. The two measures are highly correlated.

The evidence reviewed by the committee suggests that research can, in principle, measure whether police reforms can support basic tenets of and potentially improve the ROL. The committee identified candidate measures that satisfy requirements of basic face validity and are regularly produced for multiple countries over multiple years.

Many of the indicators in the V-DEM survey reflect specific components of indicators in the WJP indices. However, there are no explicit questions in the V-DEM survey distinguishing civil from criminal justice, or order and security. In contrast, the WJP survey does not explicitly ask about gendered rights or about white-collar crime by government and private officials, nor does it distinguish between higher and lower courts.

In order to validate the measures, we run two simple analyses. First, we correlate V-DEM and WJP indices; the idea is that a high correlation would offer face validity. Second, we explore whether the ROL Index captures which countries are more likely to violate human rights.

---

[1] See https://worldjusticeproject.org/our-work/research-and-data/wjp-rule-law-index-2020.
[2] See https://www.v-dem.net/en.

Using the last year for which the two leading sources (V-DEM and WJP) have data, Figure A-1 below shows a rather high correlation (0.81) between the two composite indices, which is reassuring.

In further analyses, we compare V-DEM's index, since it has a broader country coverage than the WJP index, to a measure of human rights violations. We use the Latent Human Rights Protection Scores constructed by Fariss, Kenwick, and Reuning (2020).[3] As Figure A-2 makes clear, there is a strong positive and significant relationship between V-DEM's Rule of Law Index and a country's human rights score.

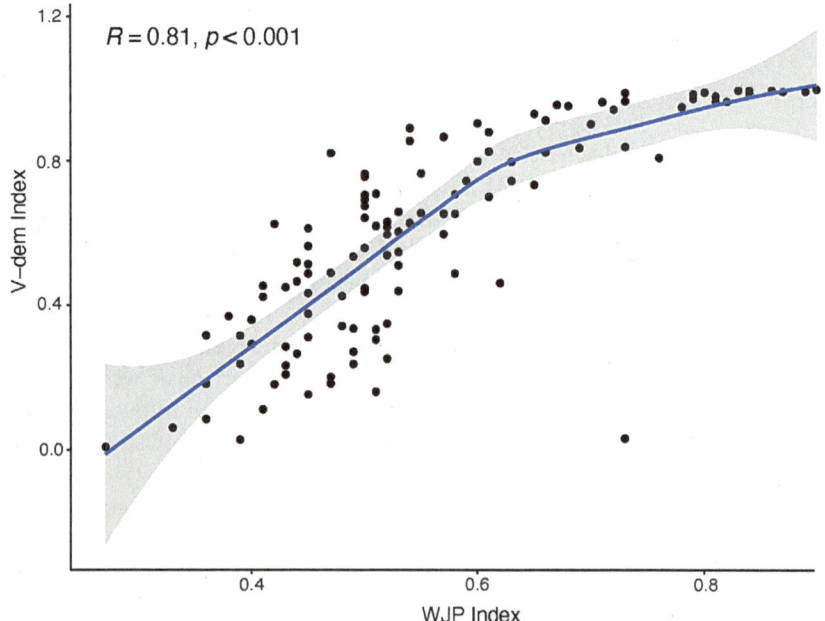

FIGURE A-1 Correlation between ROL Indexes of WJP and V-DEM, 2020.
NOTE: Each dot represents a country, with the x-coordinate its WJP ROL Index value and the y-coordinate its V-Dem ROL Index value (data source: https://www.v-dem.net/en/data/data/v-dem-dataset-v111/). In total, there are 118 countries represented in the figure that match between the 128 countries in WJP data and 179 in V-Dem data.

---

[3] The Latent Human Rights Protection Scores can be found at https://dataverse.harvard.edu/dataverse/HumanRightsScores.

APPENDIX A

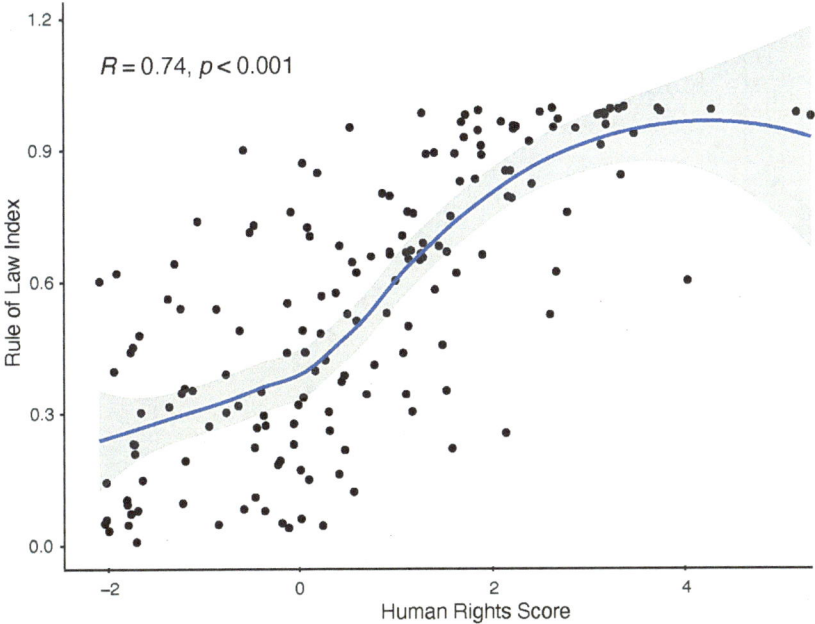

FIGURE A-2 Correlation Between ROL Index and Human Rights Scores.
NOTE: Each dot represents a country, with the x-coordinate its human rights score (data source: https://dataverse.harvard.edu/dataverse/HumanRightsScores) and the y-coordinate its V-Dem ROL Index value (data source: https://www.v-dem.net/en/data/data/v-dem-dataset-v111/). In total, there are 170 countries represented in the figure that match between the 194 countries in the human-rights-score data and 179 in V-Dem data.

Correlates of the Rule of Law

In this section, the correlates of the ROL are explored with no causality claims made: the goal is more modest, and limited to correlational analysis.

While in theory the ROL and a country's level of democracy are two distinct concepts, in practice both are highly correlated, as Figure A-3 makes clear. Here, V-DEM's index of Electoral Democracy is used; it has a 0.82 correlation with the ROL Index.

The strong correlation between regime type and the rule of law is not simply a function of how V-DEM constructs both measures. Replacing V-DEM's continuous measure of democracy with Freedom House's

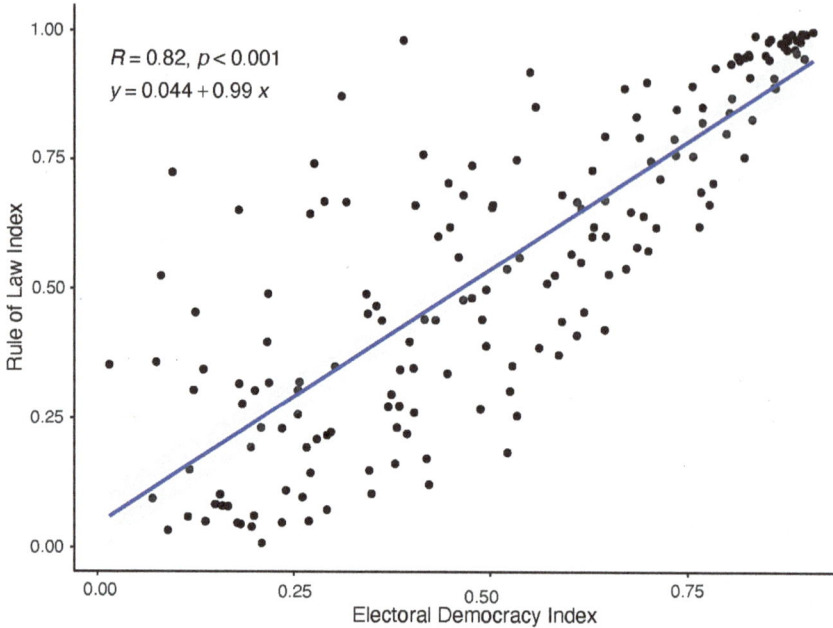

FIGURE A-3 Correlation Between ROL Index and Electoral Democracy Index, 2019.
NOTE: Each dot represents a country, with the x-coordinate its electoral democracy index, v2x_polyarchy, (data source: https://www.v-dem.net/en/data/data/v-dem-dataset-v111/) and the y-coordinate its V-Dem ROL Index value. There are 172 countries included. Note that R in the plot indicates correlation score, not R-squared for regression lines.

three-category measure of democracy (Free; Partially free; Not free),[4] a strong correlation is again found between regime type and the rule of law; see Figure A-4.

Interestingly, the strong positive correlation between a country's level of democracy and its commitment to the rule of law is observed at all income levels. Using the World Bank's income designation,[5] we disaggregate Figure A-3 to three categories: high-income, middle-income, and low-income countries. As Figure A-5 shows, a positive correlation between a country's

---

[4] See https://freedomhouse.org/report/freedom-world.
[5] See https://datahelpdesk.worldbank.org/knowledgebase/articles/906519-world-bank-country-and-lending-groups.

APPENDIX A

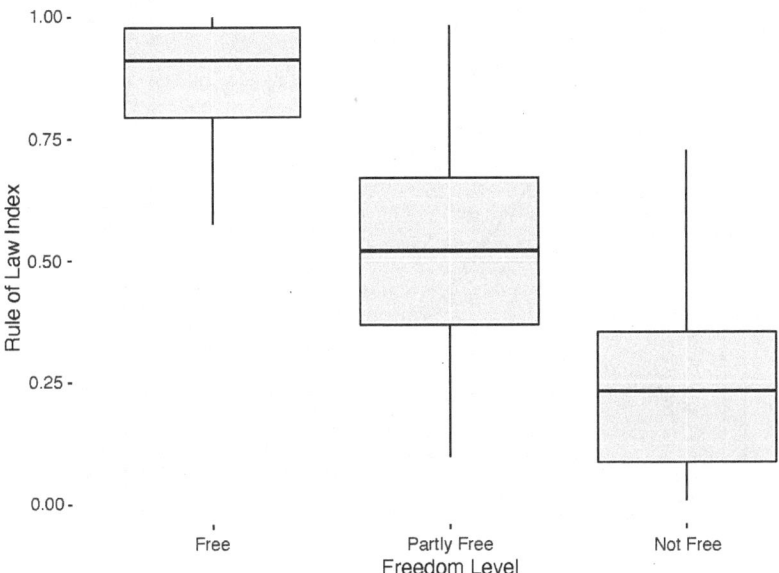

FIGURE A-4 ROL Versus Freedom Level.
NOTE: There are 175 countries included. Freedom level data from Freedom House measure of democracy (https://freedomhouse.org/countries/freedom-world/scores).

level of democracy and the rule of law can be observed at all income levels (though it is admittedly weakest for low-income countries).

Figure A-5 strongly suggests that a country's wealth is correlated with the rule of law independent of a country's level of democracy. We explore this correlation in Figure A-6, which examines wealth per capita. As the figure illustrates, with few exceptions, on average, richer countries exhibit stronger commitment to the rule of law.

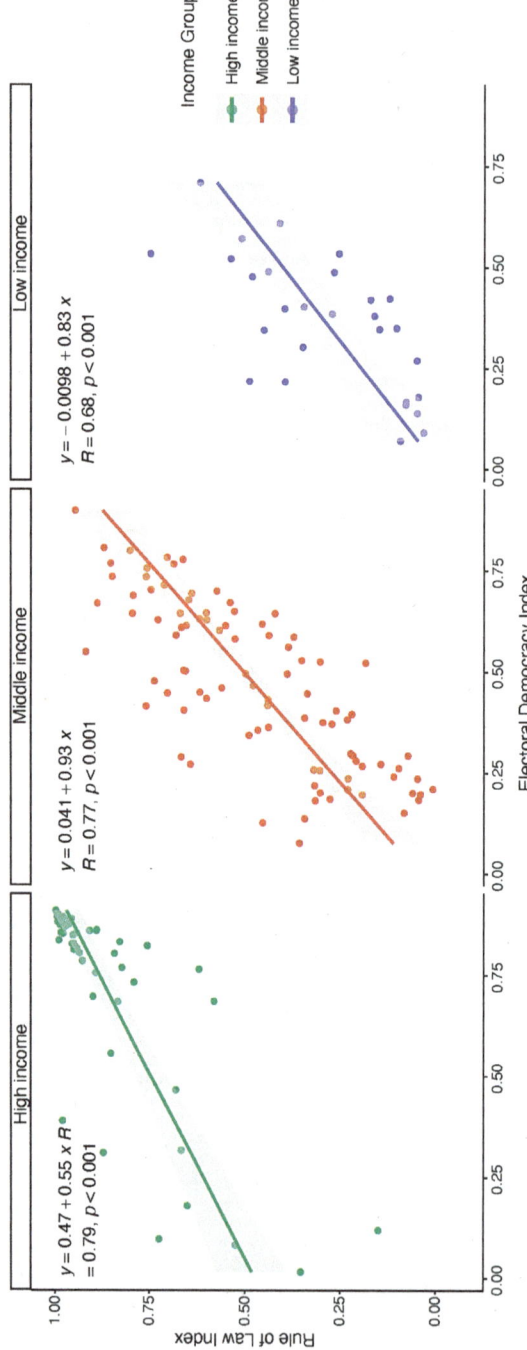

FIGURE A-5 ROL and Electoral Democracy Index, by income groups.
NOTE: Each dot represents a country, with the x-coordinate its electoral democracy index, v2x_polyarchy, (data source: https://www.v-dem.net/en/data/data/v-dem-daaset-v111/) and the y-coordinate its V-Dem ROL Index value, subgrouped by World Bank's income designation. There are 172 countries included. Note that R in the plot indicates correlation score, not R-squared for regression lines.

APPENDIX A   *101*

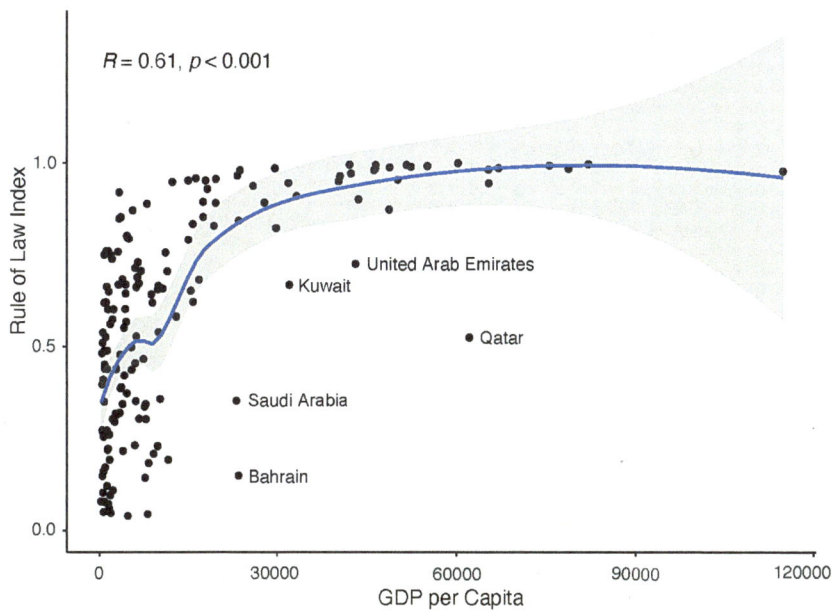

FIGURE A-6 ROL and GDP per capita, 2019.
NOTE: Each dot represents a country, with the x-coordinate its GDP per capita in 2019 (data source: (https://api-worldbank-org.proxy.library.upenn.edu/v2/en/indicator/NY.GDP.PCAP.CD?downloadformat=csv) and the y-coordinate its 2019 V-Dem ROL Index value. There are 162 countries included.

Appendix B

Biographical Sketches of Committee Members and Staff

Lawrence W. Sherman (*Chair*) is the Wolfson professor of criminology (emeritus) and director of the Police Executive Programme at the University of Cambridge Institute of Criminology. He previously served as head of the criminology departments at Cambridge, University of Pennsylvania, and University of Maryland, and as president of the American Society of Criminology, the American Academy of Political and Social Science, and the Academy of Experimental Criminology. He has designed or led more than 50 randomized field experiments in police agencies on three continents, which formed the basis for his leadership of the global professional movement for evidence-based policing, notably through the U.K. Society for Evidence-Based Policing and its counterparts in Australia, Canada, New Zealand, and the United States. He has advised governments on police policy and trained senior police leaders in multiple countries. As one of six authors of the report to the U.S. Congress *Preventing Crime: What Works, What Doesn't, What's Promising*, he wrote the chapter Maryland Scientific Methods Scale for rank-ordering the strength of evidence from impact evaluations, which has been adapted by a number of governments for their "what works" agendas on crime prevention. He has edited two volumes of the *ANNALS of the American Academy of Political and Social Science* on police and violence, most recently on reducing fatal police shootings. Sherman earned his Ph.D. in sociology from Yale University.

Beatriz Abizanda is a senior specialist in the citizen security cluster of the Inter-American Development Bank (IDB). Her professional experience spans the private and public sectors in Latin America and Europe. She has led the design, implementation, and technical advisory of major IDB criminal justice reform projects in the citizen security sector. Her projects include police modernization, prison reform, and youth-violence prevention components for programs in Belize, Brazil, Colombia, Costa Rica, Ecuador, and Uruguay. She has also coauthored the IDB's conceptual framework and operational guidelines for citizen security and coexistence and contributed to the World Bank's World Development Report. She is currently conducting meta-analytic research on the effectiveness of interventions for domestic violence perpetrators. She is a member of the jury of the Stockholm Prize in criminology and is on the editorial board of the *Journal of International Criminology*. Abizanda received an M.A. in criminology from the University of Cambridge and an MBA from Georgetown University.

Emily Backes is associate director of the Committee on Law and Justice in the Division of Behavioral, Social Sciences, and Education at the National Academies of Sciences, Engineering, and Medicine. She has served as study director for the reports *The Promise of Adolescence: Realizing Opportunity for All Youth* and *Transforming the Financing of Early Care and Education*. She is currently the study director for the Committee on the Assessment of Health Outcomes by Birth Settings. In her time at the National Academies, she has directed studies and provided analytical and editorial assistance to projects covering a range of topics, including juvenile justice, policing, forensic science, illicit markets, science literacy, science communication, and human rights. Backes received an M.A. and B.A. in history from the University of Missouri, specializing in U.S. human rights policy and international law. She also received a J.D. from the University of the District of Columbia, where she represented clients as a student attorney with the Low-income Taxpayer Clinic and the Juvenile and Special Education Law Clinic.

Yanilda María González is an assistant professor of public policy at the Harvard Kennedy School. Her research focuses on policing, state violence, and citizenship in democracy, examining how race, class, and other forms of inequality shape these processes. Her book *Authoritarian Police in Democracy: Contested Security in Latin America* studies the persistence of police forces as authoritarian enclaves in otherwise democratic states, demonstrating how ordinary democratic politics in unequal societies can both reproduce authoritarian policing and bring about rare moments of expansive reforms. Previously, she was an assistant professor at the School of Social Service Administration at the University of Chicago and has worked at a number of human rights organizations in the United States and Argentina, including the New York Civil Liberties Union, and Equipo Latino

Américano de Justicia y Género. González received her Ph.D. in politics and social policy from Princeton University.

Guy Grossman is professor of political science at the University of Pennsylvania. His research is in applied political economy, with substantive focus on governance, migration, security, and conflict processes. He is founder and co-director of the University of Pennsylvania's Development Research Initiative, a member of the Evidence in Governance and Politics network, faculty affiliate of Stanford's Immigration Policy Lab, and the University of Pennsylvania's Identity & Conflict Lab. He designed and carried out field studies in a large number of developing countries, in collaboration with various international agencies, including the World Bank, the U.K. Department for International Development, the U.S. Agency for International Development, as well as with African governments and local nongovernmental organizations. His work has appeared in *Proceedings of the National Academy of Sciences*, the *American Political Science Review*, *American Journal of Political Science*, *International Organization*, and *The Journal of Politics*, among other journals. Grossman received his M.A. in political philosophy and LL.B. in law from Tel-Aviv University and a Ph.D. in political science from Columbia University.

John L. Hagan is the John D. MacArthur professor of sociology and law at Northwestern University, and his primary areas of expertise are in criminology, criminal justice, and international criminal law. He is a member of the National Academy of Sciences and fellow of the American Academy of Arts and Sciences and the Royal Society of Canada. He is best known with coauthor Alberto Palloni for their mortality estimate of the Darfur genocide published in *Science* and his book coauthored with Wenona Rymond-Richmond *Darfur and the Crime of Genocide*. He is also the author of *Who Are the Criminals? The Politics of Crime Policy from the Age of Roosevelt to the Age of Reagan* and with Bill McCarthy *Mean Streets: Youth Crime and Homelessness*. He has received the John Simon Guggenheim Foundation fellowship, the Stockholm Prize in criminology, the Harry Kalven Prize from the Law & Society Association, and the Cesare Beccaria Gold Medal from the German Society of Criminology. Hagan received his M.A. and Ph.D in sociology from the University of Alberta.

Karen Hall is deputy executive director at the Rule of Law Collaborative. Previously, she was associate professor and director of the master of law program in democratic governance and rule of law at the Ohio Northern University Pettit College of Law. She also served with the U.S. Department of State in its Bureau of International Narcotics and Law Enforcement

Affairs. While there, she directed the development and management of assistance to the criminal justice system in Afghanistan as part of the overall U.S. foreign assistance initiative. She has also developed programs dealing with institutional reform, access to justice, protection of women's rights, and legal education. She has lived at the U.S. Embassy in Kabul, Afghanistan, where she directly managed the State Department's criminal justice and corrections programs. In recognition of her work, she earned multiple meritorious and superior honor awards from the State Department. Her teaching interests include international rule of law reform, international law, comparative criminal law, rule of law program design and management, student externship courses and introduction to the American legal system. Her current research involves examining the consequences of the appropriations and administrative processes of the U.S. government in relation to rule of law reform worldwide. Hall received an M.A. in security studies from Georgetown School of Foreign Service and a J.D. from Harvard Law School.

Cynthia Lum is a professor of criminology, law and society, and the director of the Center for Evidence-Based Crime Policy at George Mason University. She is a leading authority on evidence-based policing—an approach to policing reform advocating that research, evaluation, analysis, and scientific processes have "a seat at the table" in law enforcement policy making and practice. Her research focuses on improving law enforcement patrol and investigative operations through rigorous field research and evaluations. She has also developed numerous tools and strategies to translate and institutionalize research into everyday law enforcement activities. She is the author of *Evidence-Based Policing: Translating Research into Practice*, one of the leading volumes on the subject. She has trained thousands of police officers in the United States and around the world on evidence-based policing strategies and approaches, including for the State Department's International Law Enforcement Academy. Lum received a Ph.D. in criminology and criminal justice from the University of Maryland, College Park.

Emily Owens is a professor of criminology, law, and society as well as economics at the University of California, Irvine. She studies a wide range of topics in the economics of crime, including policing, sentencing, and the impact of local public policies on criminal behavior. Her research examines how government policies affect the prevalence of criminal activity, as well as how agents within the criminal justice system, particularly police, prosecutors, and judges, respond to policy changes. She is engaged in ongoing research projects on police training, alcohol regulation, immigration policy, and local economic development programs. Owens received her Ph.D. in economics from the University of Maryland, College Park.

APPENDIX B   *107*

Sarah Perumattam is a senior program assistant with the National Academies of Sciences, Engineering and Medicine's Committee on Law and Justice and Board on Children, Youth, and Families. Her undergraduate research focused on disaster relief and humanitarian response, culminating in her senior capstone project *Improving HIV/AIDS Treatment in Humanitarian Response: Lessons Learned from Rwanda*. She served as an international teaching assistants' consultant at Brown's Center for Language Studies and studied abroad in Seoul, South Korea, where she worked as a guest editor for the Yonsei University Annals. Perumattam graduated from Brown University with a bachelor's degree in public policy and a specialization in government, law, and ethics.

Julie Anne Schuck (*Study Director*) is a program officer at the National Academies of Sciences, Engineering, and Medicine. She has provided analytical, administrative, and editorial support for many studies and workshops and served as a technical writer for many reports. Her projects have covered a wide range of subjects, including law and justice issues; national security; STEM (science, technology, engineering, and mathematic) education; the science of human-systems integration, workforce development, and the evaluations of several federal research programs. Notably, she was part of the staff team that supported the committee that produced the report *The Growth of Incarceration in the United States: Exploring Causes and Consequences*. Schuck has a B.S. in engineering physics from the University of California, San Diego, and an M.S. in education from Cornell University.

Justice Tankebe is a lecturer in criminology and a fellow at St. Edmund's College, University of Cambridge. Prior to his current appointment, he was a teaching associate on the Police Executive Programme at the Institute of Criminology, Cambridge. His research interests lie in policing, legitimation and legitimacy, organizational justice, corruption, vigilantism and extra-legal punishment, comparative criminology, sociology of law, crime and criminal justice in sub-Saharan Africa. Tankebe's current research projects include legitimacy and counter-terrorism policing, corruption among prospective elites, sentencing decision making in Ghana, the death penalty in Africa, and police self-legitimacy. Tankebe received his Ph.D. in criminology from the University of Cambridge.

Jessalyn Brogan Walker (*Study Director through June 2021*) is a program officer with the National Academies of Sciences, Engineering, and Medicine's Committee on Law and Justice. Prior to joining the National Academies, Walker was a programs officer at the Global Center on Cooperative Security. In this position, she worked with international police trainers, officers, and leadership to promote a community-oriented approach to policing throughout their organizations. She led in the development and delivery of curriculum to be incorporated into national-level police academies in Jordan, Kosovo, Nigeria, and Tanzania. She also previously worked at the United States Institute of Peace, where she organized and delivered a host of workshops and trainings on the subject of countering violent extremism with law enforcement, government, and civil society actors. Her research interests include international root causes of crime and violence, global prison and police systems, and identity sensitivity and appreciation. She is coauthor of the book *Community-Oriented Policing for CVE Capacity: Adopting the Ethos through Enhanced Training*. Walker holds an undergraduate degree in sociology and politics and a master's degree in criminology from University College Cork.